*A Treasury of*

# CONTEMPORARY HOUSES

# A Treasury of

# CONTEMPORARY HOUSES

*Selected by the Editors of*

*Architectural Record*

PUBLISHED BY F. W. DODGE CORPORATION, NEW YORK

COPYRIGHT 1954 BY F. W. DODGE CORPORATION

F.W. DODGE

CORPORATION

Library of Congress Catalog Card Number: 54-11607

# Introduction

House design today is in a state of delightful confusion. Confusion because ideas seem to change so rapidly, or maybe because there are so many ideas, so many new things to work with. Delightful because we want our houses to be delightful. You might even say that delight is the current fashion.

Our forefathers—unnumbered generations of them—might laugh at the idea of delight being a current fashion. The age-old summary of architecture speaks of "commodity, firmness and delight." But it is still true that architecture has newly discovered the word, or at least has new visions of its realization.

It is important to realize that this represents a step forward, not backward. When contemporary architecture, many years ago, began sweeping out the sentimental litter of by-gone styles, it was going forward. It was recognizing that ancient styles, beautiful as they were in their day, were anachronisms in our time. They were merely stage settings. They did not satisfy our intellect, and if they satisfied our emotions, weren't we a little mixed up?

So architects set about developing an architecture that would satisfy our sharpened intellects. They began developing new forms, new materials and techniques, new esthetics, new combinations of space, new ways to design houses for their purposes.

What's new is not the negation of all that, it is rather the conscious effort to use it all for the delight of man's soul. It's as simple as that.

A noteworthy result is variety. And what could be more delightful in house design than variety? Why should a modern house have to have a flat roof? Or a glass wall? Or an open kitchen? Why should it have to have its structure exposed? Why shouldn't it have anything its owners really want, including a curve or two, even a Victorian curve?

Well, that's where modern architecture is today. That is why, incidentally, there is much variety in the houses in this book. All are modern. All were considered good enough to publish in ARCHITECTURAL RECORD. All are very recent selections. But not all take their academic theory in the same doses. What's more to the point, all have ideas in them, and nowadays there is no dogma, intellectual or otherwise, against using whatever ideas may appeal to you.

**Emerson Goble**

**Managing Editor**
**Architectural Record**

# Contents

**1**
**Carl Koch and Associates (see page 2)**

V IEWING CURRENT house architecture in a broad, objective sense one could easily find himself mumbling about "confusion." And, if he happened to feel in a negative mood, he could dwell upon certain inadequacies in the "modern" approach to house design; he might cite, with wrinkled nose, the supine acceptance of the cliché, and work himself into a nice tizzy.

On the more positive side, were he disposed toward cheerfulness, he might find much to nourish that mood. He might observe, for example, that the cliché work was done, as always, by the followers, not the leaders; he might even find grounds for encouragement in the fact that new ideas were

# HOUSE DESIGN: STRESSING "DELIGHT"

gaining ground in this familiar way. He might then observe that much creative work was also being done. With his eyes thus turned upward, he would certainly find architects to whom the principles of contemporary design meant creative freedom, not restrictive dogma. He could find architects to whom the sweeping away of Victoriana did not mean sterile emptiness but rather preparation for new delights to go along with the "commodity and firmness." He might then, in exalted mood, mount his soapbox and proclaim that modern architecture was moving forward in many new and exciting and delightful paths. He might even shout, "Confusion? Let's have more of it."

For the following pages, RECORD editors have selected houses that must give their owners a full measure of "delight."

**2**
**John Funk, Lawrence Halprin (page 6)**

**3**
**George Fred Keck, William Keck (page 12)**

**Edward D. Stone, Karl J. Holzinger, Jr. (page 16)**
**4**

**Richard Gordon (page 20)**
**5**

# DEVELOPING THE "DELIGHT" OF A VERMONT SITE

*Residence for Mr. and Mrs. James Parton, Dorset, Vt.*

*Carl Koch and Associates, Architects*

IT WOULD BE DIFFICULT to find a house that better illustrates the freedom of the contemporary architect to develop the theme of "delight" with full sympathy for the wishes of the owner and the assertive regional character of the site. The "restriction" placed by the owner was "that the house should not conflict in its appearance too radically with its local surroundings or in such a way that the conservative Vermont residents would throw up their hands in horror." The architect continues, "the house was designed to fit the slope of the existing mound to the southwest of the dam and was to be built on three levels. . . . We used a slightly pitched roof and board and batten siding both because of our own preference and in order to give the house a Vermont character."

Property is the site of an abandoned marble-cutting mill, comprising six and a half acres at the south end of a 15-acre pond. Mill is long since gone, but the dam of marble remains, and brook is faced with marble blocks

At upper level, living room is cantilevered out over the brook. House follows contours as it recedes from the dam, dining room and kitchen being a few steps lower than living room, bedrooms at a still higher level

*Fireplaces and floors in dining and living rooms are of native marble from the site, also the terrace at dining-room level. House was built for all-year living, and has radiant heating coils in the floor.*

# DESIGNED FOR BOTH FOREGROUND AND BACKGROUN

*Residence for Mr. and Mrs. John Woerner, Kentwoodlands, Cal.*

*John Funk, Architect; Lawrence Halprin, Landscape Architect*

*A. Curley Henrickson, General Contractor*

Morley Baer

This house both defies its overwhelming site and defers to it, while developing its scenic possibilities to the full. The defiance may be seen in the assertive manner in which the house takes its own form, perhaps also in its insistence on a close-in landscaped beauty spot for outdoor living as well as for bowing to Mt. Tamalpais or scanning San Francisco Bay. The distant views are nevertheless terrific, and the house and its gardens together certainly do not neglect those stimulating items. The landscaping still develops the pleasures of myriad growing things, of paved terraces for both adult and children's outdoor enjoyment, for full participation with the outdoors. The landscaping offers both profusion and variety to delight the eye, and then, working outward from the house, tends to blend imperceptibly with the distant landscape.

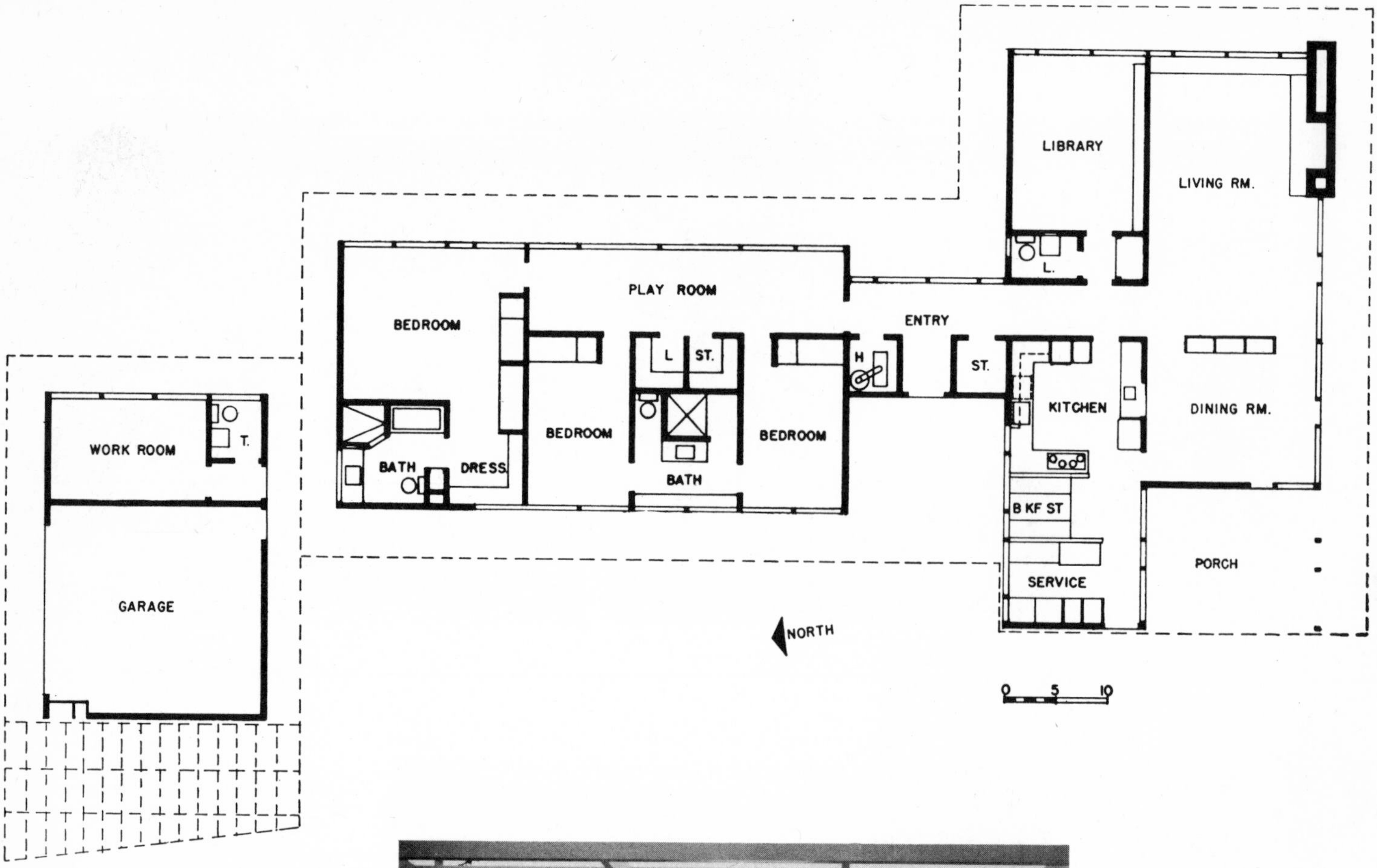
LIBRARY
LIVING RM.
L.
PLAY ROOM
ENTRY
BEDROOM
L
ST.
H
ST.
KITCHEN
DINING RM.
WORK ROOM
T.
BEDROOM
BEDROOM
BATH
DRESS
BATH
B KF ST
PORCH
SERVICE
GARAGE
NORTH
0
5
10

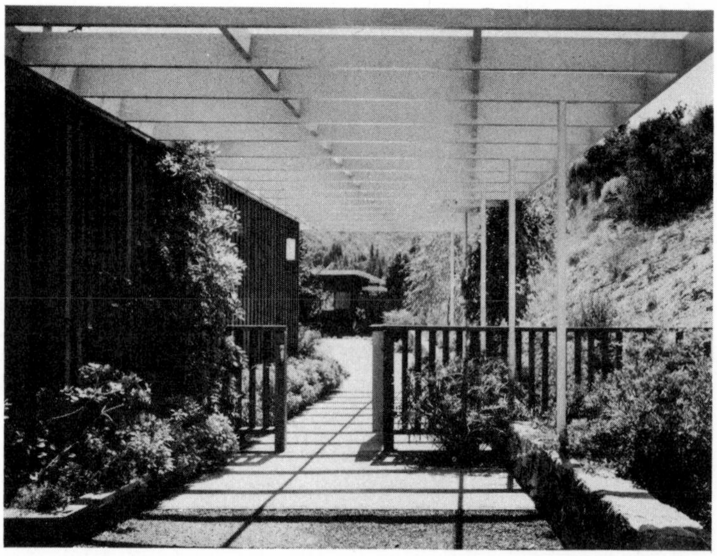

Morley Baer

WOERNER HOUSE

*A partly sheltered walkway leads (above) from parking court to entrance, with wisteria climbing the garage wall. Closer to the entrance (below) the walk widens into landscaped court*

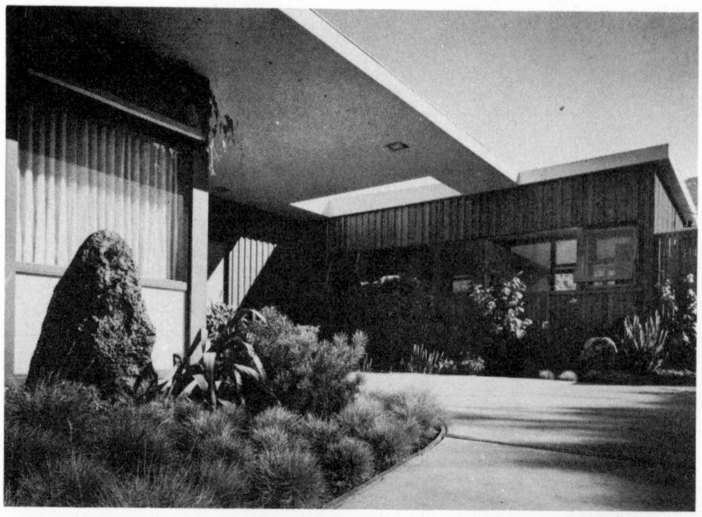

House interiors, if more formal and severe than the gardens, have the graciousness of great spaciousness. Living room looks out at that all-pervading mountain, is partially screened from dining room by cabinets. Both dining and living room have plenty of glass facing the views. Bedroom wing faces the Bay, with low plantings in foreground, small trees off a bit farther to frame the view toward the water

Morley Baer

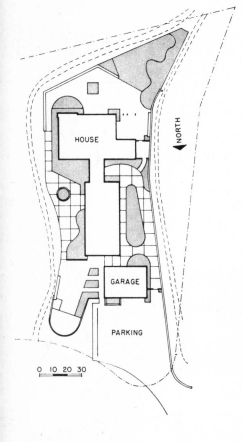

Glass walls open the house to an intricate arrangement of paved terraces and garden beds and lawns. Many of the outdoor "rooms" are connected, sometimes by walks, sometimes only by planting boxes or beds. Other areas are closed off for privacy or for utilitarian purposes by board fences. There is seemingly endless variety in the plantings — flowers, shrubs, trees, grasses, vines. There is variety, too, in paving materials, in garden rocks and walls, in beds and stands, in colors and textures of inert and growing materials. But the varieties are blended and integrated by choice of textures and forms. Colors are also used in continuous blends and gradations to achieve continuity and to make the whole recede gradually into the hillsides.

# AN INNOVATION IN OPEN PLANNING

*Residence for Mr. and Mrs. John C. Telander, Hinsdale, Ill.*

*George Fred Keck, William Keck, Architects*

If anybody doubted the "delights" of modern architectural thinking, a single feature of this house might dispel his gloom. The view opposite shows the lower portion of a two-level living room, with a playful stairway joining the two portions, and with a two-story glass wall offering a truly huge view of the woods. This innovation in open planning the architect designates in his notes as two different spaces — living room and recreation room. One can imagine, however, that on occasion the two would flow together more actively than in the visual sense only. In general the house does not seem to bow to style, unless creativeness itself is a style.

Hedrich-Blessing

*Bedroom wing is isolated from the rest of the house by a large entrance foyer (above) which, with its brick walls, stone floor, and planting, gives a sense of being outdoors, strengthening the feeling of separation*

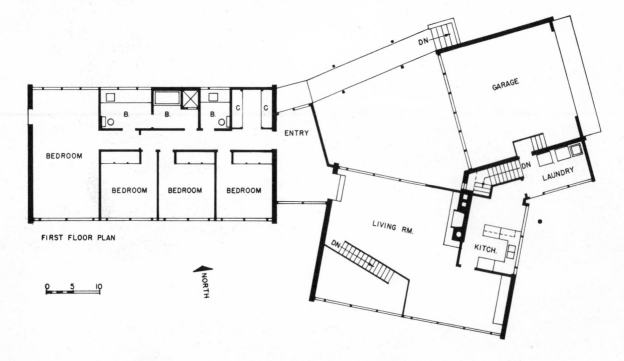

FIRST FLOOR PLAN

0  5  10

NORTH

Hedrich-Blessing

*Dining room, as an open extension of the living room, has its own identity, but still adds to the spaciousness of the living room. Thus three spaces — dining, living, recreation — flow together spatially but still maintain their individual purposes*

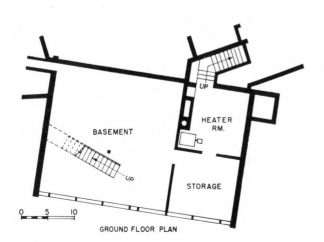

BASEMENT

HEATER RM.

UP

UP

STORAGE

0    5    10

GROUND FLOOR PLAN

# HOUSE DESIGNED TO WARM THE WINTER SCENE

*Residence for Mr. and Mrs. Fred Maduro, Great Neck, Long Island*

*Edward D. Stone, Architect; Karl J. Holzinger, Jr., Associate*

Ben Schnall

What the client really wanted here was a tropical house on Long Island, and the architects have managed to transplant a number of tropical features, or at least reminders, without doing violence to the essential conditions. Without, moreover, merely contriving a stage setting. The owners, born in Panama, found New York winters especially trying, and the house subtly woos them to an enjoyment of the winter scene. There is a sense of protection, for example, in wide overhangs, which, psychologically if not physically, keep the snow and ice farther from the house. There is the same sense in the enclosed patio, itself a feature dear to the Latin-American heart. Radiant heat made its own contribution. And indoor planting certainly is a subtle reminder of a warmer clime. Perhaps more important than these more tangible things, however, is a general charm in the interiors — the fireplace wall, for example — which could scarcely be called romantic but which are obviously warm and appealing.

*Main entrance is through enclosed patio. House has many subtle*
*features to remind owners of their birthplace, Panama*

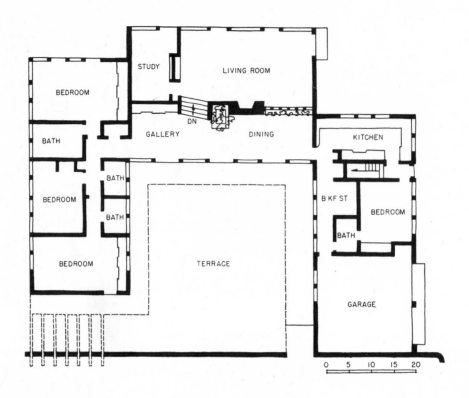

*Patio enclosed at the front by 6-ft brick wall provides a sheltered area for outdoor living as well as privacy from driveway. Full height windows are used along dining gallery, high windows for bedrooms and bathrooms. Wide overhang is reminiscent of Latin-America, tends to keep snow away from glass walls*

*Library and living room look out toward pond. A frozen pond makes a cold winter scene, but the Latin-American owners say that in their new house they enjoy cold winters for the first time in the years they have lived in the north*

Ben Schnall

# CONTEMPORARY HOUSE IN COLONIAL SETTING

*Residence for Mrs. Edward Pearson, Mamaroneck, N. Y.*

*Richard Gordon, Architect*

The house pictured above does not look Colonial, and it certainly makes no pretenses in that direction. However, from the other side (opposite page, top) all one sees from the road is a carport and a blank white brick wall, this in deference to a generally Colonial neighborhood. The other side (above) is virtually all glass, facing a river that runs through the property. Here the house develops its own delights. The architect explains that the owners asked him to act as contractor in order to use some fairly inexperienced carpenters who were available. Thus the house is designed for especially simple construction. It is laid out on a 4-ft 3-in. module, with 6 by 12-in. long leaf yellow pine beams. The beams rest in steel straps welded to light structural steel T columns imbedded in the poured concrete foundation. Beams are 8 ft 6 in. on center, so that 4 by 8-ft mahogany ceiling panels would go in place without cutting.

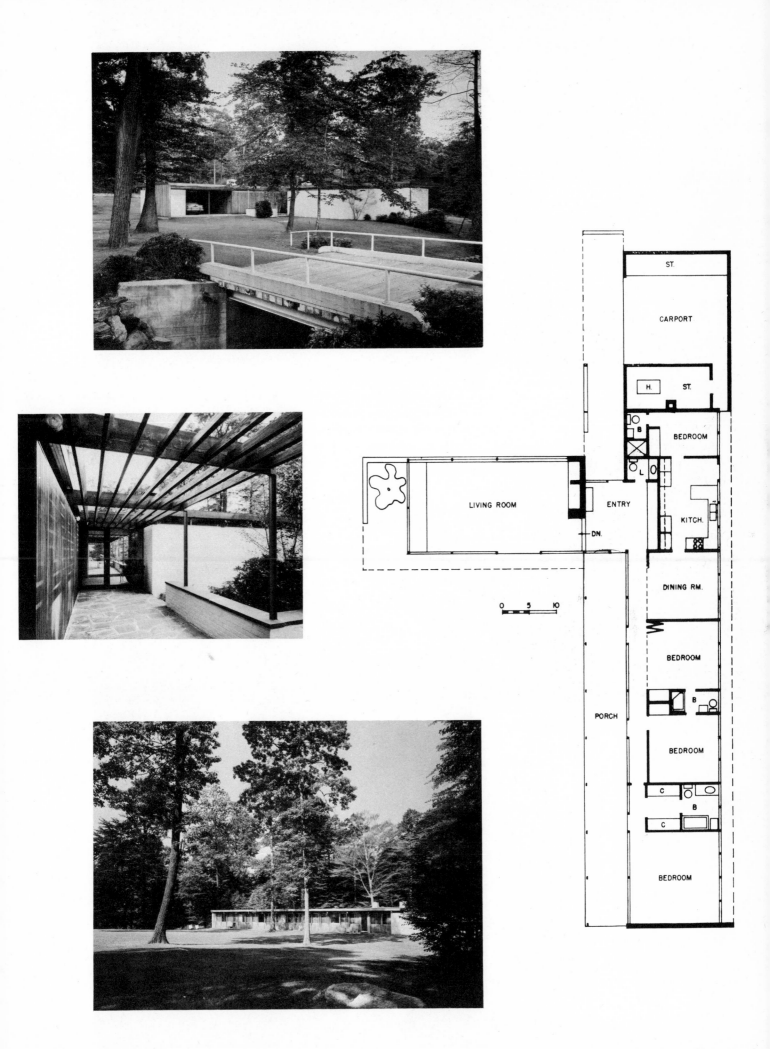

ST.

CARPORT

H. | ST.

B | BEDROOM

LIVING ROOM | ENTRY

DN.

L

KITCH.

DINING RM.

0  5  10

BEDROOM

B

PORCH

BEDROOM

C

B

C

BEDROOM

© Ezra Stoller

*L-shaped form of house screens terrace at living room and lawn sloping down to the river that runs through the property. Long porch on bedroom wing with trellis-type roof is useful for outdoor dining or for any other purposes that porches are for*

*Living room is completely open on river side, completely closed on road side,*
*with only shallow light windows between the roof beams*

*Planting bed at far end of living room merges the indoors with the outdoors.*
*Living room wall extends beyond and makes turn to screen room fully from road*

*Dining room is positively removed from living room, is in fact part of bedroom wing; kitchen is behind entrance foyer without a door, thus disposing of any idea of eating in living room*

© Ezra Stoller

# FOR HOUSES—OPEN OR CLOSED PLANNING?

THE VIRTUES OF THE OPEN PLAN have intrigued us all for quite a while, and stirred up a lot of arguments. By now, few can seriously question that it is a good method for gaining flexibility and a sense of space in today's smaller, more compact houses — and perhaps for lowering the cost. Public acceptance is gaining ground, too, with some of the consumer press leading with such glibly assured phrases as "The house these photographs were taken *through* . . .". But even a virtue can be overworked and used indiscriminately, at the sacrifice of other desirable qualities. There are certainly some individuals who would rattle around by themselves in an open-plan house, some who would be rattled by the more or less frenzied activities of others in a family group. There are many ways, some old, some fairly new, of combining both advantages of space and privacy: three houses are presented here that were designed to be used open or closed.

Joseph W. Molitor

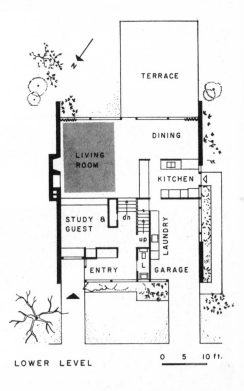

LOWER LEVEL          0   5   10 ft.

OPEN OR CLOSED PLANNING?

## 1. In Suburbia: equal demands on space and privacy

*Cambridge, Mass.     Carleton R. Richmond, Jr., Architect*

SITE LIMITATIONS and close-by neighbors can pose rather acute problems in many typical residential areas. In planning his own house, Carleton Richmond was faced with zoning restrictions limiting building width to 38 ft, and with a six story apartment house looming to the rear of his 150-ft-deep lot. The resulting compact design incorporates a variety of devices to give the occupants (a couple and one child) privacy from the neighbors, and an interior plan which can be as open or closed as desired. All living areas form a single large room, with plan elements carefully articulated by changes in ceiling and floor levels, and by movable partitions. Obscured glass shields the front entry, while glazing at the rear is protected by a large canopy and trellis.

An illusion of space is created by downstairs open plan, though rooms are small. For privacy, surrounding rooms can be shut off from living area (gray area on plan). Study (right) doubles as an office, also as guest room

Joseph W. Molitor

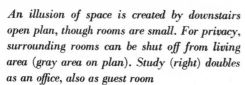

Living room becomes part of garden when lower glass sections are raised (mechanism is similar to sketch, right). The spatial quality of the room can be altered in varying degrees by different arrangements of opening walls, folding partitions, blinds and curtains. Kitchen is closely integrated with dining and living rooms but may be completely shut off from both

BEARINGS CENTER ON COLUMN
WORM GEAR
CHAIN
MOVABLE DOUBLE GLASS
REMOVABLE CRANK
ANGLES SET INTO BASEMENT WALL
(FLOOR)
WEIGHT

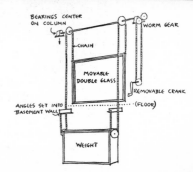

ROOF

TERRACE BELOW

UPPER STUDY - LIVING RM.

MASTER BEDROOM

dn

B

STOR.

BEDROOM

0  5  10 ft.

UPPER LEVEL

Joseph W. Molitor

*Storage walls in bedrooms form sound barrier against living room. High windows in master bedroom help ventilation, privacy*

*Trellis members over terrace and trees are spaced to restrict view from apartment house at rear, yet pass winter sun and view of sky*

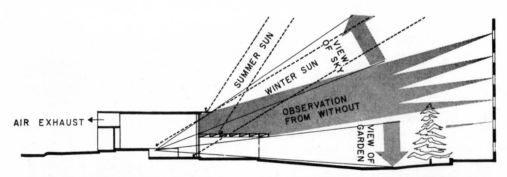

AIR EXHAUST ←

SUMMER SUN

WINTER SUN

VIEW OF SKY

OBSERVATION FROM WITHOUT

VIEW OF GARDEN

## 2. In Resorts: the setting is the capital, seclusion a profit

*Honolulu, T.H.   Lemmon, Freeth & Haines, Architects*

APART FROM open-interior considerations, in surroundings as magnificent as Hawaii the average client is usually willing to trade a fair loss of privacy for a series of views. But any protection against the prying eyes of the curious and the tourists is a welcome asset. In this house for Dr. and Mrs. T. W. Cowan, roadside planting and a steep slope have been used to give considerable seclusion to the small terrace and big window at the front of the house.

R. Werkam

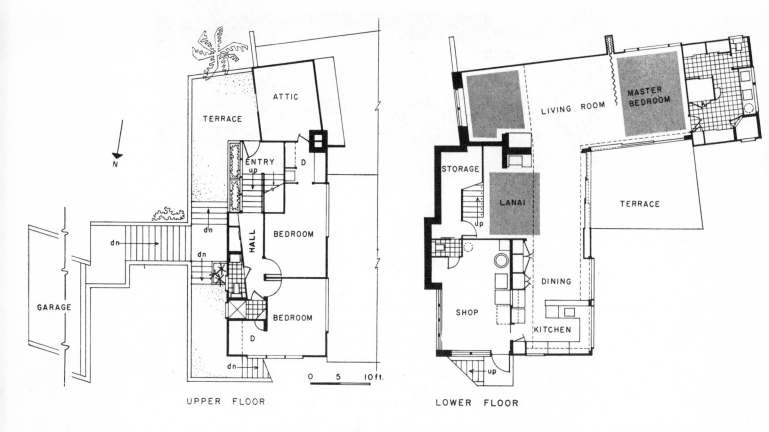

UPPER FLOOR                 LOWER FLOOR

**RESORT HOUSE: HAWAII**      *A fairly unusual plan disposition provides all facilities for the owners at the lower level in an open arrangement, with extra bedrooms, each with dressing room and lavatory, and a split-bath on the upper floor*

*Open as it is, the lower level of the house does provide some corners for retreat in the alcoves and closeable bedroom (gray areas on plan). All dressing facilities for the bedroom adjoin the compartmented bath. The terrace may be closed off with sliding glass or screen panels. Deed restricted placement of house on lot so views of neighbors' houses aren't blocked*

# 3. In the Country: interior flexibility gains importance

*Austin, Texas   R. Gommel Roessner, Architect*

A CLIENT with a near-rural or rural site will sometimes demand a house flexible enough to entertain, feed and sleep a small army of guests or relatives from time to time, and yet be snug and efficient when just the family is present. A paragon somewhat along these lines has been achieved in this house for Mr. and Mrs. Millard Rudd on the outskirts of Austin. Both the living areas and children's room adapt to various arrangements.

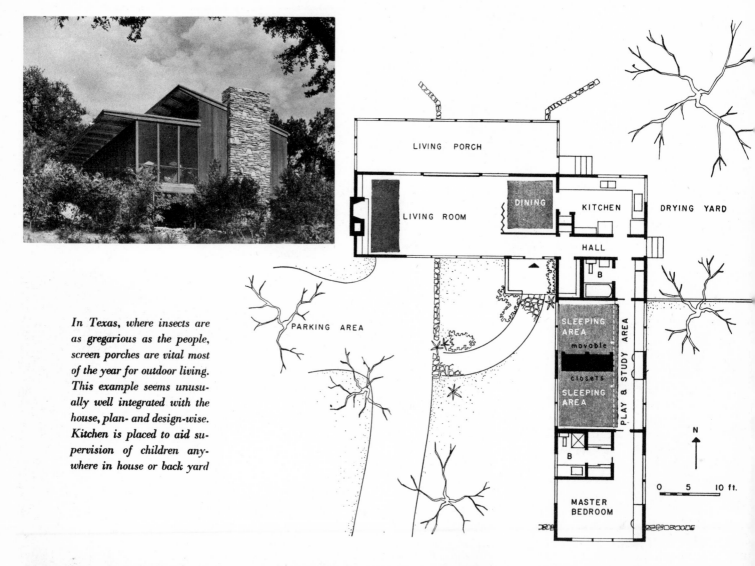

*In Texas, where insects are as gregarious as the people, screen porches are vital most of the year for outdoor living. This example seems unusually well integrated with the house, plan- and design-wise. Kitchen is placed to aid supervision of children anywhere in house or back yard*

*The children's room (right) is designed as an extremely flexible unit. A portable closet partition and reed curtains make it easily convertible from a single large room into three separate areas. Convenient rear door and bath help prevent children's tracking mud through house*

*The extra space added to living room by porch and
dining area gives ample room for large groups.
Fireplace end retains closed-in feeling. Wall between
dining area and entry is louvered for ventilation*

Mears

*Residence of Mr. and Mrs. Norton Polivnick*
*Denver, Colorado*

*Norton Polivnick, Architect*

*Gerald F. Kessler, Landscape Architect*

# VERTICAL EXPANSION PROVES ADVANTAGEOUS

THIS HOUSE was originally designed for a family of three, with provision for guests and probable family expansion; the requirements were flexible, but the budget was not. The architect-owner based his plan on maximum use of every inch of space: the living-dining room, for instance, could be used also as a drafting room, guest room or music center; kitchen, laundry and both bedrooms were held to moderate size, and as much furniture as possible would be built in. When more room was needed, extension of the bedroom wing would be simple and economical.

Before the time for expansion had come, however, a new and large house had been built close by on the adjoining lot. The Polivnick house, with its extremely low roofline (ceiling height, 7 ft 4 in.), was lost among its neighbors, and additional height was badly needed to restore the balance. Expansion would have to be vertical, not horizontal as anticipated.

**January 1954**

*Original house was dwarfed by new neighbors; addition of second floor restored balance. Exterior walls are cedar predipped shakes and vertical T & G siding*

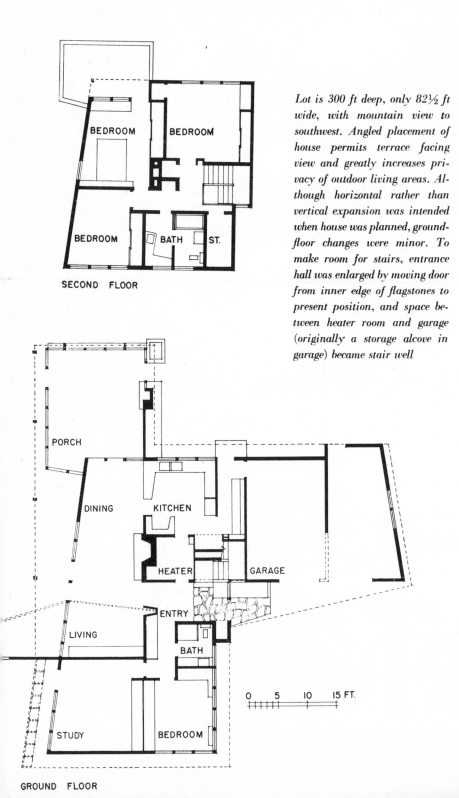

BEDROOM BEDROOM

BEDROOM BATH ST.

**SECOND FLOOR**

*Lot is 300 ft deep, only 82½ ft wide, with mountain view to southwest. Angled placement of house permits terrace facing view and greatly increases privacy of outdoor living areas. Although horizontal rather than vertical expansion was intended when house was planned, ground-floor changes were minor. To make room for stairs, entrance hall was enlarged by moving door from inner edge of flagstones to present position, and space between heater room and garage (originally a storage alcove in garage) became stair well*

PORCH

DINING KITCHEN

HEATER GARAGE

ENTRY

LIVING

BATH

STUDY BEDROOM

0   5   10   15 FT.

**GROUND FLOOR**

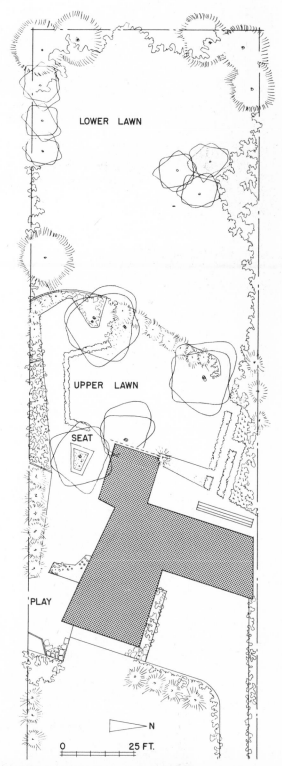

LOWER LAWN

UPPER LAWN

SEAT

PLAY

N

0   25 FT.

## VERTICAL EXPANSION PROVES ADVANTAGEOUS

As things turned out, a second story proved to be not only possible but actually advantageous. The original plumbing stack, hot water boiler and chimney could serve the new second floor; the existing roof became the sub-floor of the addition; and all new bearing walls were related to existing exterior walls. Whereas the cost of the original house had been $15 per sq ft, the cost of the 900-ft addition was about $7 per sq ft.

*When second floor was added dining room terrace was converted into a screened porch. Roof overhang along living room (below) previously had been extended to its present width with trellises and columns (top left, opposite page)*

Barbecue fireplace is now within area of screened porch; it is only a few steps from kitchen. All interior walls on first floor are knotty cedar vertical T & G, cabinet work is fir plywood, floors are concrete with asphalt tile finish, ceilings are plaster tinted an off-white to blend with natural finish of wood. On second floor, all finish is mahogany, floors are hardwood (carpeted), and ceilings are painted gypsum board

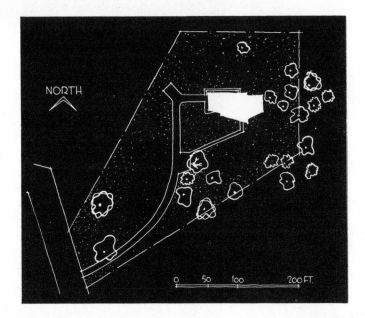

# DESIGNED FO

*House for William E. Neume*
*Du Page County, Illin*

Extending brick cavity walls beyond glass plane expresses the three-part plan and supports overhangs. Precise orientation for maximum solar effect. Top and bottom ventilation through screened louvers

# NFORMAL LIVING

*orge Fred Keck–William Keck, Architects*

GARAGE  DINING  K  UTILITY  DRESS'G

DK.R.

TER.  LIVING  BR  BR

ENTRY

NORTH

0 5 10 20 FT.

The open living-dining-kitchen area gives the guest at table a pleasant sense of "being near the kitchen" while still enjoying the view

Hedrich-Blessing

THE OWNERS REPORT, "we are experiencing a most comfortable and relaxed life in our . . . house. Satisfying esthetically and for ease of maintenance."

A sense of openness is achieved by sloping the roof up to the south over large glass areas and by a single space for living-dining-kitchen. This almost U-shaped area is wrapped around the owner's darkroom and abuts the utility room. In a maidless household, such an arrangement allows host and hostess to chat with their guests while preparing drinks and dinner.

The wood frame is supported by brick cavity walls; ceilings are acoustical plaster; interior walls brick, plaster or birch plywood; floor is cement finish over circulating hot water radiant heating coils.

NEUMANN HOUSE

*In master bedroom, built-in birch wardrobe divides sleeping and dressing areas. Fluorescent tubes at top of cabinet provide indirect room lighting and also illuminate contents through glass*

Hedrich-Blessing

1. **Hugh Stubbins, Architect**

# 3 HOUSES

*Each Designed to Meet the Problems of its Specific Setting*

A HOUSE designed for its particular site, capitalizing on the environmental advantages and minimizing the shortcomings in the surroundings, seems such an obvious and natural solution when one builds — yet the percentage of residences so conceived is undoubtedly shockingly small. Architects have only scratched the surface as far as volume of residential work is concerned; but herewith are three examples showing the lasting benefits of complete architectural service.

There is a Massachusetts house designed to overlook a river in two directions; a residence on a flat, treeless plot in a built-up neighborhood in Alabama; and a home on a secluded rock ledge in the Connecticut hills. Three disparate properties, each holding a house tailored to a specific scene.

2. **Sherlock, Smith & Adams, Architects**

3. **Joseph Salerno, Architect**

Joseph W. Molitor

P. E. Guerrero

# 1. THE VIEW SHAPED THIS HOUSE

*Hugh Stubbins, Architect*

THE HIGHLY SUCCESSFUL two-way character of the living area, below, came about in gaining a view of the Charles River in two directions. The outside stair to the dead-level roof, p. 41, was requested by the client for the same reason. The unusual free-standing fireplace is built of stone and plaster.

Study of the plan and photographs will reveal several points worth noting: living, dining and principal bedrooms oriented to the view, with bedrooms set apart for privacy by a plan recess and wood slat screen, bottom photo; the long entrance hall, photo below plan, which separates study and workshop from living and can be entered from the garage; the central kitchen, located adjacent the children's play court and drying yard for control and access; the orderly organization of the plan elements within a modular post and lintel structural system, which is in turn frankly expressed in the finished house, both inside and out.

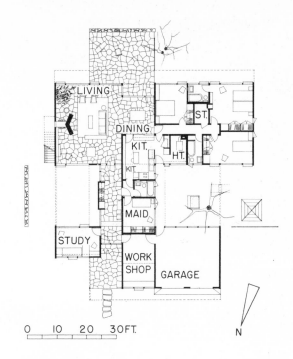

0    10   20   30 FT.

N

*Weston, Massachusetts*

© Ezra Stoller

The photo immediately below shows the cheerful dining area and its adjacent terrace for outdoor dining with the river view. The kitchen divider is a two-way pass through cabinet, bottom photo, finished in natural redwood with sliding panels of obscure glass and plastic. The kitchen, left, achieves balanced light and ventilation from a clerestory and the windows opposite.

On the right page, bottom, is a view of the court between living area and study, top photo. This pleasant in-and-out and tying-together relationship is enhanced by the device of carrying through the modular lintel for structural expression and unity.

## 2. TRADITIONAL NEIGHBORHOOD AN

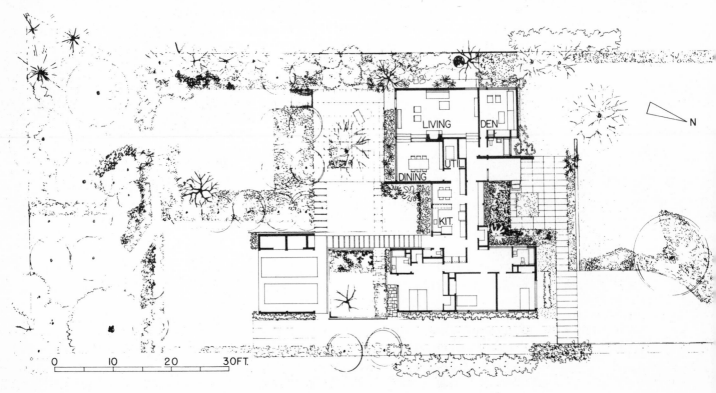

0    10    20    30 FT.

## REELESS LOT

The Samuel P. Baum Residence,
Montgomery, Alabama

Sherlock, Smith & Adams,
Architects
Charles M. Kelley, in charge

Edward L. Daugherty,
Landscape Architect

Bear Brothers, Contractor

LOCATED between two-story traditional houses in an established neighborhood on a plot devoid of trees, this house (see plan) makes the best of its situation. Principal rooms are located to face the south, or off-street portion of the site and to overlook a terrace and sunken garden. A deed restriction forbidding a garage "at the front of the house" led to removing the future carport south of the master bedroom to create a screened garden between.

The scheme stretches the living, service and sleeping zones across the plot; placing the kitchen between the other two zones makes it not only a noise buffer, but in addition a convenient control point for the children's indoor and outdoor play.

Joseph W. Molitor

Both the living and dining areas orient south for privacy and winter sun, as does the master bedroom. Materials: pink brick, cypress in natural finish, painted plaster, striated plywood in natural finish; floors of carpet, plastic tile, oak, or flagstone.

*The elevation to the west is shown below. The east facade, above, is divided by the entrance loggia, at right*

P. E. Guerrero

# 3. ON A ROCK LEDGE IN THE WOODS

*The Fromkin House, Westport, Conn.*

*Joseph Salerno,* Architect

*James Fanning,* Landscape Architect

*Richard Goemann,* Heating Engineer

*Charles Cornell,* Foreman

THE ARCHITECT put it quite well when he said, "The central idea was to do as little as possible to a beautiful site. Here was a rock ledge in a secluded area overlooking a small park of lovely trees to the south. Locating the house on the ledge required no study whatsoever; from the points of view of approach, elevation, view, orientation, and the best trees, there was no other possible location for it.

"All of the landscaping was executed with material that was already growing there or might have been. Hemlock, laurel and azalea are the basic plants, with vinca minor used as ground cover. There are no 'gardens' or 'lawns' in the usual sense."

The plan is essentially three more or less enclosed blocks disposed to define a large living area. The entrance is a court or loggia between these elements.

For clearer spatial definition, the living room is subdivided by fireplace seating and the large mass of the fireplace and by built-in bookshelves. Such a scheme furnishes space for reading, music and also occasional large scale entertaining as well. The room seems comfortable whether it contains two or thirty. The considerable amount of natural light is supplemented by artificial light from incandescent tubes, which yields a pleasant effect. From any spot, one is constantly aware of the magnificent wooded view.

**3. ON A ROCK LEDGE IN THE WOODS**

*The pitched-roof promontory above the
living room both trusses the greater
span and yields gable-end cross light*

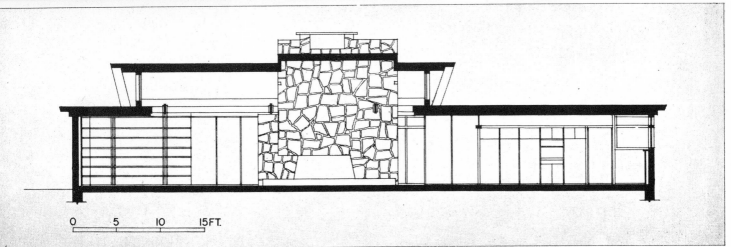

Music  Reading          Conversation                    Dining      Kitchen

*The added height sets the living area
apart as a flexible, multi-use space
which dominates the entire composition*

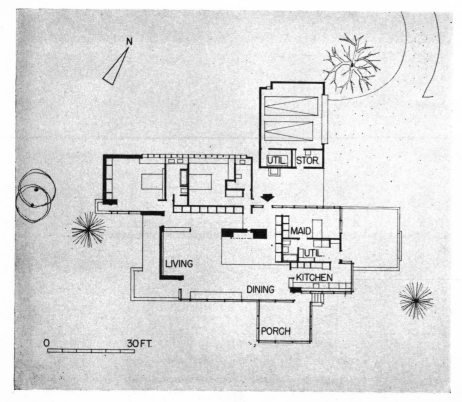

*The two photos, this page, look southwest to the park and southeast through the dining area to the porch*

0       30 FT.

*The kitchen, two views above, boasts windows to the south and southeast. Note especially the large number of built-in features in all areas of the house; this is true also in bedrooms, photograph below*

# PLANNED FOR CHILDREN

## *The Frederic Wieting House,*
### *Swampscott, Mass.*

*Carl Koch & Associates, Architects*
*Frederic L. Day, Jr., Associate*
*John F. Carey, Contractor*

THE PROBLEM OF PLANNING living and growing-up space for four children under six as well as for an older son who pays frequent visits was a basic requirement of the program; important also was to provide for easy control of the children's area from the kitchen and space for the parents' privacy, as well as facilities for undisturbed adult entertaining. A one-level scheme was a further request of the clients.

The plot commands a sweeping view of the ocean to the south and east and is less wooded, more suburban in character than architect Koch had encountered before. Since the terrain sloped gently south to the sea and was bounded west and north by streets, it was decided to place the house broadside to the view with access to the garage from the west.

Initially one parent favored a modern design while the other was opposed; even to a conservative version. The house as built has a pleasing character that incorporates many of the best aspects of both schools, and has completely won over the dissident partner.

*The principal facade, which opens south to the view, is shown above and at right. Some exterior walls are vertical natural cedar siding; others are painted cinder block. Thick-butt asphalt shingles protect the roof. Photo at left looks from terrace into the jalousie-sheltered dining porch*

# THE WIETING HOUSE

© Ezra Stoller

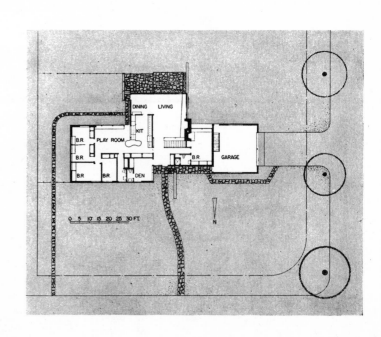

*View of living room looking towards entrance hall, above. The
free space about the two-sided storage unit separating living
room and stairway visually expands the otherwise small entry*

*The plan might be described as a "corridorless" one which re-
volves about the playroom-kitchen-laundry-family dining area
which serves as a center for control and housework and also as
a main passage. The small basement, required by the owner,
worked out well, and this experience has led the architect to
favor basements as a practical solution for storage, shop, or
even living space; provided the terrain has a natural slope*

Normally the entire family gathers around the built-in table in the kitchen-laundry-playroom area at mealtime, and the adult dining room is used principally for entertaining guests. The playroom is oriented south to the ocean view and opens directly upon the childrens' play area, visible from the kitchen. Glazing in the high gable provides additional natural light

Bedrooms for the two boys nearly of an age are divided by a flush wood sliding partition, below at left. The master bedroom, below at right, is oriented south with lateral protection for quiet and privacy provided by the living room wing, and is located at the minimum distance from the children's wing necessary for seclusion. Stock sliding aluminum windows

# FOUR-ZONE PLAN FOR GRACIOUS LIVING

### *The Sigmund Kunstadter House, Highland Park, Ill.*

*George Fred Keck and William Keck, Architects*
*Marianne Willisch, Interiors*
*Raymond M. Hazekamp, Landscape Architect*
*Walter J. Olson, Builder*

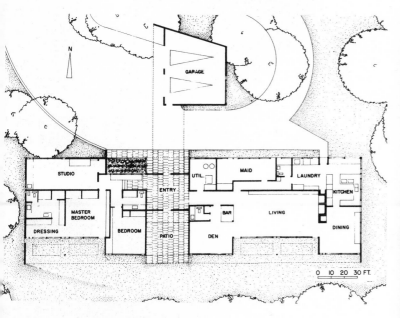

Winner of the 1953 Honor Award for the Best House Design, Chicago Chapter, A.I.A., this suburban home captures a measure of the graciousness many have come to associate with older houses and combines it with the more informal, open character typical of to-day's plan. After stepping from his car under the porte-cochère which links house and garage, the guest enters a large, glass-enclosed central hall from which he may be received in the studio-library for quiet talk, in the living area for a family or party visit, or may be shown directly to his guest room (normally the den) to freshen up before making an appearance.

At first glance the rooms appear to be rather freely disposed in plan, with interesting "ins and outs" for the long façades, but closer analysis reveals a studied arrangement which places these elements within a rectangular structural cage consisting of eight uniform bays. Note how this rectangular form is maintained by an unbroken fascia on posts which continues even where the garage walk roof slides under it.

*The four plan zones (car maneuvering and garaging to the north; living, dining and entertaining to the southeast; service and utility to the northeast; quiet study and sleeping to the west) are articulated with and arranged about the central hall to provide: proper entrance, exit and service; convenient interplay of elements and flow of space for desired privacy without isolation; informal living without confusion*

Wood is used for the exterior and much of the interior finish; straight grained cedar with a modicum of pigmented paint in the preservative so the grain and tone are revealed but uneven interim discoloration is prevented. Other interior walls are white plaster. Ceilings are acoustic plaster. Floors in important areas are cork; in other areas vinyl; in the entry slate. Large fixed sash are double-glazed; the ventilators consist of weather-stripped inside doors, fixed screening and wooden louvers. An interesting feature is the large masonry mass, limestone faced, containing living and dining area fireplaces and also an incinerator which is fed from the utility room.

*The large entry, left page, is a focus for the entire scheme. View of living area, above, looking over the built-in sofa towards the den-guest room, bar and entry. The bar is concealed by a vertical sliding panel (shown raised in these pictures). Architect-designed suspended lighting fixtures house continuous tubes as well as a trolley duct for spots to highlight owner's paintings*

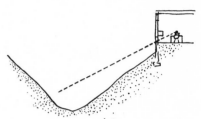

*The glass panels below the dining room cabinet, left, provide a view into the wooded gulley to the east. The lower photo shows the kitchen area and space for informal eating beyond the cabinet*

Hedrich-Blessing

The manner in which the principal rooms relate to the outdoors and to the sun and seasons was an important consideration in the design. Large transparent walls for these spaces that open to the south are sheltered by both overhangs and extended solid vertical planes to give from within both openness with privacy and a strong sense of protection

Master bedroom, top photo, features a headboard designed by the architects, as well as a long wardrobe closet (not shown). The opening leads to the adjoining dressing room and bath, shown in the center picture. The L-shaped, plastic-topped lavatory counter contains two units and is both backed up by and flanked by long wardrobe units. There is also a stall shower, tub, and an enclosure for toilet and bidet. The bottom photo pictures the studio-library, which is oriented to the north for good light. The lower cabinet against the far wall contains both a sink and storage

# ARCHITECT'S HOUSE BUILT IN TWO STAGES

*Residence of Mr. and Mrs. Robson Chambers*

*Palm Springs, California*

*Clark and Frey, Architects; Robson Chambers, Partner*

HERE IS A HOUSE WELL PLANNED at the outset to meet the changing needs of a young couple. Small and compact at first, it was easily enlarged several years after it was built, when the size of the family was increasing. At that time the new master bedroom suite shown in the plan opposite was added, the porch was enclosed in obscure glass to form a dining room, a sun bathing patio off the three bedrooms was closed off with an aluminum and redwood fence 6 ft high, and a double carport was built.

Living room and bedrooms have large glass areas on the south to admit winter sun and a wide roof overhang to shut out the hot summer sun. All major rooms open to the outside through 8-ft-wide sliding glass doors. The house is fully insulated, air cooled and electrically heated. Construction is wood frame.

*Photos opposite and below were taken before house was en-
larged and grounds were landscaped; see next page for recent
view of exterior. Oleander hedges form separate outdoor courts*

Julius Shulman

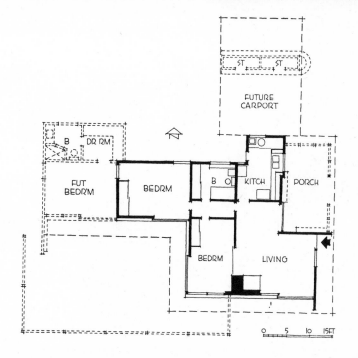

## CHAMBERS HOUSE

*Left above: flexibility of living room is increased by sliding plywood panel between it and guest room. Left: roof is so framed that no lintels appear over sliding glass doors, but ceilings carry outside unbroken. Under side of overhang is corrugated aluminum*

*Opposite and below: high aluminum and redwood fence now closes off sun bathing patio. These new photos show how the additions and landscaping have carried original design of house to completion*

Julius Shulman

*Residence of Mr. and Mrs. A. W. Duvel*

*Omao, Kauai, Hawaii*

*Lemmon and Freeth, Architects*

# SIMPLE PLAN EXPLOIT

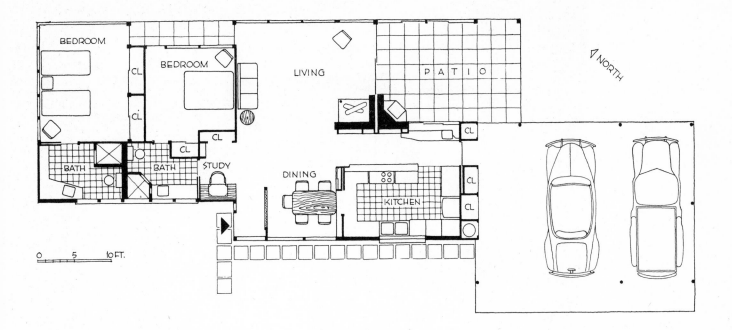

# NSPOILED SITE

SIMPLICITY of plan and structure plus an unspoiled natural site mark this small house on the northern-most island of Hawaii.

The plan is the simplest possible answer to the owners' requirements — living-dining room, patio with barbecue and bar, study, two bedrooms and two baths. It is, moreover, as open as consistent with privacy: there are only two full-height partitions in the entire living area, one between the living room and the son's bedroom, the other the short brick chimney wall. The master bedroom is connected with the rest of the house only by the lanai; the son's room, however, intended for future guest room use, opens through its bath to the study alcove as well as directly to the lanai.

Construction is wood frame on concrete foundation. Single-board walls are 1¼ by 12-in. redwood T & G, stained on exterior, stained and waxed on interior. Roof is composition on exposed rafters and 2½-in. thick cane fiberboard sheathing. Floors are colored concrete except in bathrooms where asphalt tile is used.

The site is large, remote from the main road, and has a sizable stream flowing through it. The stream was dammed to form a pool which, with broad lawns surrounding it and a little planting close to the house, was virtually all the landscaping required. The owner, Forester for the Division of Forestry, Board of Agriculture and Forestry on Kauai, was landscape architect; his wife was decorator.

Living room, patio and lawn form one continuous living area overlooking stream
and pool. Interior walls are gray with touch of red, ceilings are blue-green

R. Wenkam

Three-part living area is tied together both actually and visually by back-to-back living room fireplace and patio barbeque, each copper-hooded and brick-walled

Dining area and kitchen are separated by two-way cabinet with pass-through

R. Wenkam

*Low corrugated plastic screen separating dining area from entrance creates wonderful feeling of openness. Kitchen (below, left) has low partitions on two sides, windows on third. Below right: study alcove*

# SLOPING SITE FOR HOUSE FACILITATES ZONED PLAN

*House for Mr. & Mrs. Ogden Kniffen, New Canaan, Conn.*

*Marcel Breuer and Eliot Noyes, Architects*

Ben Schnall

A SIMPLE, ONE-LEVEL HOUSE is comparatively easy to organize into the various kinds of areas needed; when several floors — and within these, numerous slight changes in level — are studied with a view to zoning them according to use, the problem tends to become complex. It cannot be as over-simplified as the current speculative builder's cliché, the "split-level house," yet it demands a simple solution. In this conventionally wood-framed house the organization of areas or zones is clearly apparent. Not so easily comprehended, perhaps, is the skill with which an open character has been maintained. The usual thing to do with the living room (see plan) would have been to open it to the south only; but using a change of level and a two-way fireplace to delimit the dining room, making the bedroom above a balcony, and opening the wall to the east court have made the room more livable and satisfying.

Ben Schnall

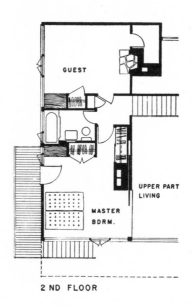

Upper floor contains adults bedrooms; lower floor has distinct zones for 1, children's play and sleeping; 2, living; 3, utility; and new bedrooms (see below)

2 ND FLOOR

GUEST

MASTER BDRM.

UPPER PART LIVING

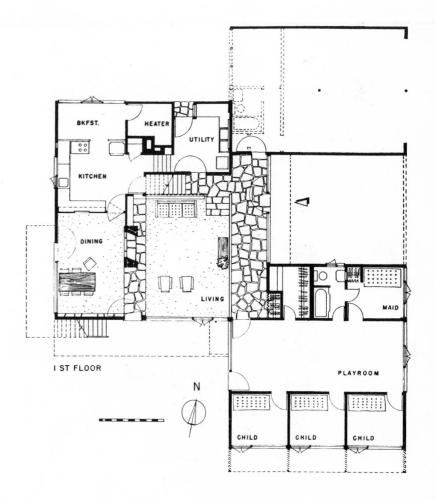

Zoned plan, characteristic of many houses by these architects and at one time a daring innovation, has here been ingeniously developed to take full advantage of the sloping site. House has been enlarged since original plan (right) was made; dotted-line area at rear of garage has become hall and powder room for access to two bedrooms, bath and storage room which extend 14 ft to north; see photograph on preceding page

BKFST.        HEATER
                          UTILITY
KITCHEN

DINING

LIVING

MAID

PLAYROOM

CHILD    CHILD    CHILD

I ST FLOOR

N

## SLOPED SITE: ZONED PLAN

The careful organization of space is accompanied by a pleasantly open interior; changes of level are advantageously employed. The diversity of interest in form thus produced is offset by the simplest of interior finishes: gum plywood, painted or natural; plate glass; solid carpeting, bluestone floors; T & G cypress

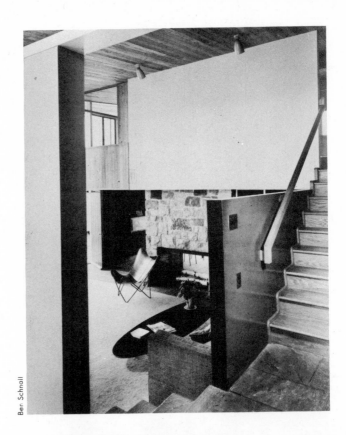

Ben Schnall

# FIVE BEDROOMS CAN BE ADDED

*House for John W. Hanson, Huntington, N. Y.*

*Marcel Breuer, Architect*

TRULY EXPANDABLE, and with the future expansion positively provided for, this house anticipates growth; change need not either prove unduly expensive or impair its original quality. The carport, which can become three bedrooms and two baths for two children and a maid, has been designed with openings ready for glazing, heating and water connections ready for extension. The playroom can be subdivided into two more bedrooms. Construction is simple wood frame on a radiant-heated concrete slab; exterior walls have vertical T & G cypress siding. The wood-framed butterfly roof roughly parallels the contours of the land, helping to fit the building into its site.

Ben Schnall

Carport and playroom of this Long Island house (shaded areas below) are designed so they can be converted into five additional bedrooms

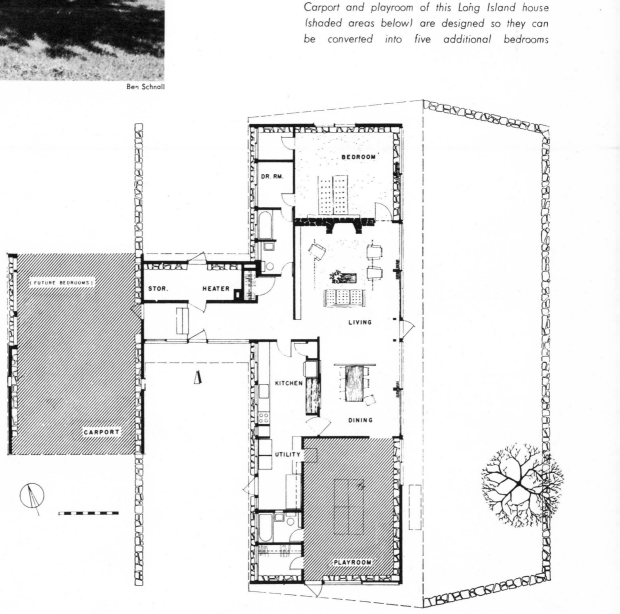

Ben Schnall

*Flagstone floor, field stone fireplace, wood ceiling and painted storage wall carry into the interior the same materials and finishes used on the exterior, heightening unity of indoors and outdoors*

Molitor

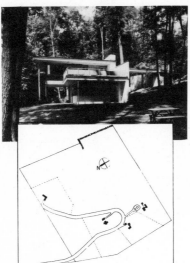

# THE HOUSE AS ARCHITECTURE

*Top: four houses, Hanover,*

*N. H., by E. H. & M. K. Hunter.*

*Bottom, l. to r.: Day house,*

*Everett, Wash., by Harold*

*Hall; Wolf house, Oakland,*

*Calif., by Campbell & Wong;*

*Wimberly house, Honolulu,*

*T. H., by Wimberly & Cook*

T SOME ARCHITECTS the house is today the best opportunity for individual expression, a fascinating problem of comprehensible size. Again, it may be a burden to be avoided if possible, or an acceptable commission only *en masse*. These seven custom-designed houses, considered together, encompass many problems typical of the field. For simplicity we have selected examples done for owners who are all professional people and hence sympathetic to the rationale of contemporary design; two are the architects' own houses. All are relatively small; all show the effects of locale, site, materials and labor; all were normally financed and most were designed with resale possibilities in mind. While all the architects concerned have indicated that in such houses there are intangible professional satisfactions, adequacy of fees, as one put it, is "debatable." Below are three houses on individual plots. Above are four designed as a group on a jointly owned jointly developed, 33-acre hillside site. All are presented in the following twenty pages both as architecture conditioned by specific locale, today's technology and owners' needs; and as instances of the professional problems that arise even in favorable circumstances.

Chas. R. Pearson

Morley Baer

R. Wenkam

The House as Architecture

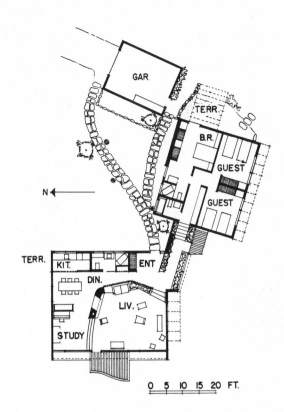

E. H. and M. K. Hunter House

E. H. and M. K. Hunter, Architects

0  5  10  15  20  FT.

# ESIGN FOR THEMSELVES

### Clients and Architects

The Hunters try to work so closely with all their clients that seldom is there a fundamental conflict. This means long conferences, mutually educational, covering not only requirements but also personalities, living habits and wishes not always easily defined. In this house of their own, though they did not face the same problems of explaining esthetic and practical matters that they naturally encountered in designing the three other houses in the group, the architects did do the same exhaustive research into their own needs. Their budget was limited, so for some time the study area served as a bedroom, partitioned off with closets which have been removed; the bedroom wing was added recently.

Joseph W. Molitor

*The architects realized that their own house would be critically regarded by clients, friends and visitors. The graciously large living area, unified by a continuous ceiling yet subdivided by stone chimney, corrugated glass and changes in floor level, makes the most of intimate views to the south and north and of the western panorama of the Green Mountains*

Joseph W. Molitor

The House as Architecture

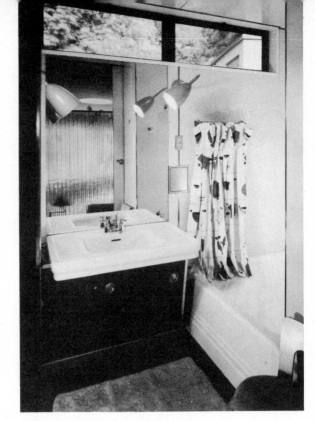

### Local Factors

In all four Hemlock Hill houses it was understood that local customs, not much changed since the days of carriages and long skirts, carried little weight. On the other hand, the demands of the region were met in careful planning for the trying climate, in large glass areas oriented south for natural heating, in liberal use of thermal insulation, and in use of flat or low-pitched roofs to hold snow and gain "free" insulation value. In these practical and esthetic effects of climate on design, the architects believe, lies true regional expression.

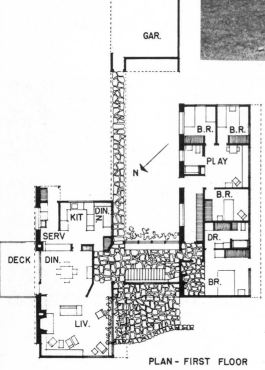

GAR.

N

B.R. B.R.

PLAY

B.R.

DR.

BR.

KIT DIN.

SERV

DECK DIN.

LIV.

PLAN - FIRST FLOOR

0 5 10 15 20 25 FT.

Like the preceding house, this one was built
in two stages. At first the downstairs study
and guest room were subdivided into bedrooms; later the bedroom wing was added

HTR.

ST.

GUEST

STUDY

PLAN - LOWER LEVEL

*E. H. and M. K. Hunter, Architects*

### Clients and Architects

All the clients on Hemlock Hill had some strong traditional architectural contact, some in the south, some in New England. Before the designing of these houses started, while the clients had a fair understanding of contemporary architecture, they recognized more fully the potentialities for improved living in a contemporary home. At the same time, each approached such matters as raising children quite differently; in this case a playroom and separate entrance were required, so toys and outdoor clothing could be kept out of other areas.

### Materials and Labor

Other than local stone and concrete block, almost no local materials were available. Despite the region's reputation as "lumber" country, good lumber comes from the far west. Consequently, three of these houses have light steel framing; and this was also found to cut costs by reducing the inefficiency of cutting and fitting wood members. Local labor is familiar with steel joists, etc., so there was no difficulty here.

Joseph W. Molitor

CHILD

B.R.

GUEST

DECK

SECOND FLOOR

*HEMLOCK HILL* | HOUSE FO

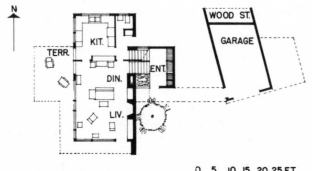

N

KIT.

TERR.

DIN.

LIV.

ENT.

WOOD ST.

GARAGE

FIRST FLOOR

0  5  10 15 20 25 FT.

Joseph W. Molitor

# R. O. SHERWIN STAPLES

*E. H. and M. K. Hunter, Architects*

In most cases, when clients on Hemlock Hill questioned unusual esthetic elements, when sound practical reasons could be advanced in their support, they were accepted. Individual preferences, however, were often the governing factor. For instance, Mrs. Staples preferred bedrooms on a second floor — and thus the house was designed; while all the others wanted direct access outdoors from master bedrooms. Again, the individual budget had dictated that the two preceding houses be built in successive stages (or else such materials as stone and acoustic plaster might have been eliminated); this and the next house were completed in one stage, though this necessitated using concrete block in the Staples house.

In none, thanks to careful programming and completely honest presentation, was design changed in fundamentals. There were, of course, some minor changes in plan which were not serious. This was the more remarkable since there was little opportunity for any of the clients to "feel out" contemporary design except in a few local houses.

## Local Factors

The four occupied sites and a potential fifth were selected and laid out by the architects, with most of the owners participating as fully as possible in determining them. All liked the land, its slopes, the large trees, the woodland character. Thus the sites, several of them steeply sloping, had a substantial effect on design. All were agreed that it was important to fit these houses to their land, to work with it to make a whole picture in use and appearance.

# HEMLOCK HILL | HOUSE FOR DR. W. C. LOBITZ

E. H. and M. K. Hunter, Architects

### Materials and Labor

This is the most recently built of the four houses. At the time of its construction, the Korean war, strikes and high cost per pound made the use of steel out of the question; it is the only one in the community that is completely wood-framed.

### Clients and Architects

This family needed four bedrooms and a study, and more conventional living, dining, kitchen and breakfast space. Furthermore, the view to the west was also to be made visible from the kitchen.

Joseph W. Molitor

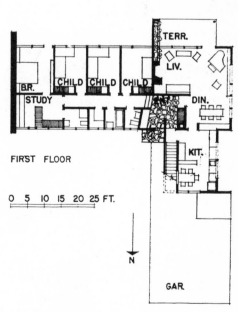

FIRST FLOOR

0  5  10  15  20  25 FT.

N

## Financial Matters

The architects believe that any house should be designed with resale possibilities in mind, since the owner's situation may change. At the same time, each of the four houses was custom-designed for its owners (a paradox which all architects face) and all four were financed with local savings bank mortgages. All these factors complicated design to some extent, increasing the countless hours of conferences required to bring design to the desired point of perfection. The standard percentage fee was felt to be a fair return, although the architects say: "This is not a field in which one can make a comfortable living: yet it is the field that affords the deepest satisfaction."

Joseph W. Molitor

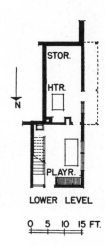

STOR.

HTR.

N

PLAYR.

LOWER LEVEL

0  5  10  15 FT.

*All four of the houses on Hemlock Hill have wood studs, built-up roofing, copper flashing, steel casements and projected sash, flush doors. All baths have plastic-surfaced hardboard on the walls. Floors are concrete slabs with little or no excavation, contain copper tube radiant panels and are surfaced with a variety of materials—asphalt tile, slate, flagstone, wood, carpet, or matting*

*EVERETT, WASH.* | # HOUSE FOR RUSSELL DAY

Harold W. Hall, Architect
Arthur A. Graves and
David W. Dykeman, Associates

### *Clients and Architects*

This very small house was designed for the head of the Junior College Art Department and his wife, who, as one would expect, highly appreciated architectural values and gave the architects utmost freedom. It was designed, on a tight budget, for a family with no children, although bedrooms can be added to the south. The clients wished to live informally, but to provide for large gatherings of friends.

Chas. R. Pearson

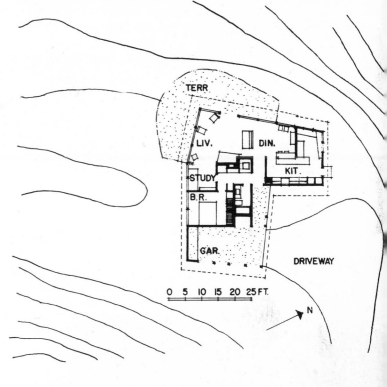

## Local Factors

There were no local customs strong enough to become design determinants, but the site is a knoll overlooking Puget Sound, which did strongly influence design. Local materials, chiefly wood, were employed, as they have been in several neighboring contemporary houses, following a recognizable regional pattern.

## Finances

The house was definitely designed with resale possibilities in mind; the possible extra bedroom was part of the original scheme. Although the architect says the owners were ideal clients and consequently matters went smoothly, he further states that a "normal" 10 percent fee did not produce an adequate return.

# HOUSE FOR HAMILTON WOLF

Morley Baer

### Clients and Architects

The owners — Mr. Wolf is an art teacher and his wife, curator of an art gallery — have an unusually high understanding of architectural matters. Both wanted a fitting modern house, and while they had a definite program they did not dictate design. Their budget was quite limited, so inexpensive materials were used and, since they needed both a working studio and a fairly spacious living room (for quite a bit of entertaining), some items of equipment have been omitted and more cubage added.

### Local Factors

The surrounding houses are mostly local "Spanish," the neighbors typically suburban. The Wolf house was designed to fit its site and, the architects say, "to blend with the pines." It is built principally of redwood.

### Finances

The house was designed not only with resale possibilities in mind (the studio can easily become a bedroom) but also with the knowledge that an F.H.A. mortgage was to be obtained. When we asked the architects if this job represented a sound use of their time and effort, the answer was: "Yes — subject for much discussion." To the question, "Did the fee represent an adequate return?" They replied: "Yes — but debatable; subject for *long* discussion."

Campbell & Wong, Architects

Eckbo, Royston & Williams, Landscape Architects

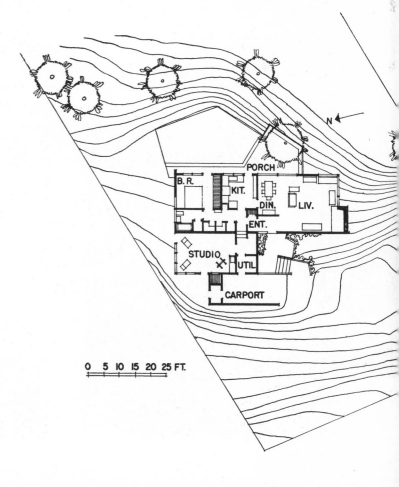

0  5  10  15  20  25 FT.

The Hamilton Wolf house is quite small and simple; its proportions were carefully studied. In particular, the relation of openings to wall areas merits inspection, and such devices as the porch or deck extending to the east increase the feeling of spaciousness

*Wimberly & Cook, Architects*

*Paul Jones, Associate*

### Client, Architect, Locale

George Wimberly, again, designed his own house; it took him eighteen months to fit it to his hillside, to devise baffles to prevent sun glare, to get the ceilings high and the windows low. He is impatient with mainland customs transplanted bodily, as they so often are, to Hawaii. He wants the climate and the local brilliance of color to be reflected in his work.

Wenkam

Although the mean average temperature locally is quite comfortable, there are times when heat builds up and the ground-level breeze could be used to advantage; hence the ceiling height, window location and sun baffles. He has also tried to make the lanai not just a concession to a quaint native idea, but an integral part of the scheme.

R. Wenkam

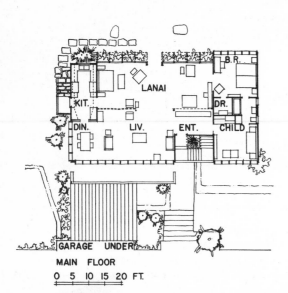

GARAGE UNDER

MAIN FLOOR

0  5  10  15  20 FT.

B.R.

LANAI

KIT.

DR.

DIN.      LIV.      ENT.      CHILD

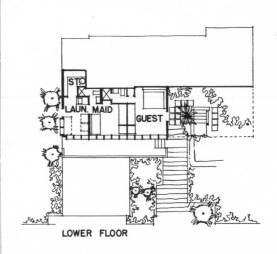

STO

LAUN. MAID      GUEST

LOWER FLOOR

*Wimberly house in Hawaii has walls of a single thickness of 1¼-in.
T & G fir, like most Hawaiian houses. Floors are maple, ohia wood, and
waxed green concrete. Living room and lanai (above) have a coral ceiling*

# RAISED BASEMENT EXPANDS HILLSIDE HOUSE

### Residence of William Wallace Landsberg, Architect
### Port Washington, Long Island, New York

FOR HIS OWN HOUSE on Long Island, William Landsberg has added several new twists to ways of gaining more real and illusionary space from a compact plan, and at relatively low cost. The hillside site was used to considerable advantage. The "basement" area was only partially set into the slope, reducing excavation costs, and providing extra usable space at ground level. This area contains a studio which can be converted into a spare bedroom and bath, storage space, a large reception hall, and an economical and convenient arrangement for the garage. The basement has, in effect, only three foundation walls, of concrete block; the fourth consists of openings and a stone veneer panel. The wood frame structure of the upper floor is cantilevered out from the ground floor, and gives protection to the openings. Fairly standard techniques were used to increase the apparent size of the living space: large, carefully placed glass areas, open planning and direct access to a terrace and ground level at the rear. Costs were reduced, however, by using exposed studs as a screen partition, ganging utilities, and dividing glass areas into smaller simply-framed units.

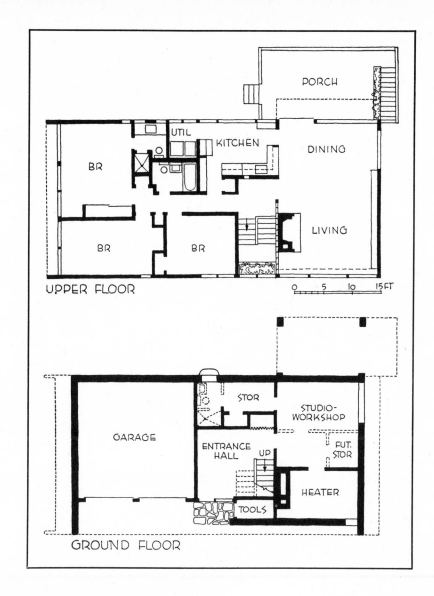

PORCH

UTIL  KITCHEN  DINING

BR

BR  BR  LIVING

UPPER FLOOR

0  5  10  15 FT

STOR

STUDIO-
WORKSHOP

GARAGE

ENTRANCE
HALL  UP  FUT.
STOR

HEATER

TOOLS

GROUND FLOOR

*Very good circulation and convenience for a servantless household
are provided for in the plan. The kitchen is placed for easy access
to both indoor areas and the porch; overlooks play yard at back*

Joseph W. Molitor

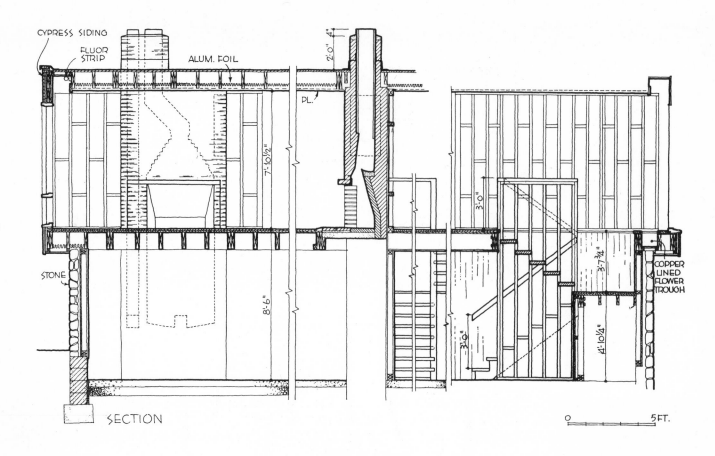

CYPRESS SIDING
FLUOR STRIP
ALUM. FOIL
2'-0" 4"
PL.
7'-10½"
3'-0"
STONE
8'-6"
3'-7¾"
3'-0"
4'-10¼"
COPPER LINED FLOWER TROUGH

SECTION

0    5 FT.

The entrance stair hall (right) gives an unexpected sense of space as the intermediate landing is reached. Sections above show details of stairs, fireplace and the exposed stud partition

Joseph W. Molitor

The quantity of large trees reduced the problem of orientation (south and east elevations shown above). The exterior has cypress siding, asbestos cement board below bedroom windows, copper coping. Most rooms have cross ventilation

Raised living room gives some privacy from entrance drive,
excellent views. The house has radiant heat in ceilings of
upper level, floors of lower level; basement floor is 4-in.
concrete slab on 6 in. of gravel

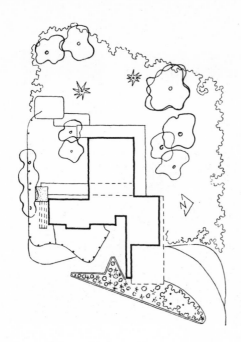

# SAFETY FOR CHILDREN—PRIVACY FOR ADULTS

*Residence for Mr. and Mrs. Samuel Sale*

*Pasadena, California*

*Whitney R. Smith, Architect*

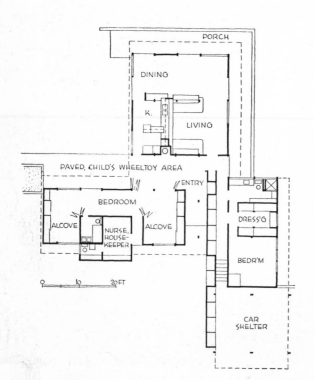

SAFETY for the young children and privacy for the parents highlight this small California house. Since neither the safety nor the privacy, nor even the combination of the two, is unusual, the chief interest here is in the skillful use of a rather small and restricted site. Had the house not been placed across the lot as it was, neither the children nor the adults would have had such complete privacy in their outdoor recreation areas; the proximity of the house to the road, however, required special treatment of the main entrance areas.

As the plans at left show, the house was divided into three separate wings: one for the children, one for the dining-living area, and one for the master bedroom suite. The children's wing is accessible only from the main entrance hall and the sheltered play terrace. The rest of the house can be reached either by a path from the street to the front door or by the more private route between carport and master bedroom wing.

House was placed across site to close off children's wing from driveway and street, and to give adult wing direct access to carport. Photos opposite: top, bedroom wing and carport; center, house from street. Left: porch around living-dining area is at ground level only at rear of house. Below: adult wings are connected with rear terrace by hall leading past cork-covered accordion doors of children's quarters

Julius Shulman

Sleeping alcoves in children's wing. are diplomatically alike in size and arrangement. Each has one whole wall of closets and cabinets—enough storage space to see any child through collecting stage. Skylights have adjustable light control

Julius Shulman

Doors separating sleeping alcoves from central play area and rest of house are accordion-type, covered with cork, and equipped with ball-bearing rollers to facilitate operation and prevent damage to cork floors; check blocks on connecting jambs keep doors from opening on straight line, eliminating need for auxiliary support. Outdoor play terrace (left) is direct extension of playroom; hop scotch and shuffle board "courts" were built into terrace slab

Entire living-dining section of house is rimmed by elevated porch protected by roof overhang. Dining area (below) is connected with kitchen by pass-through which may be opened or closed as desired. Record player and record storage unit (bottom of page) was made focal point of living room instead of more usual fireplace; built-in couches slide out, can be made up as beds. Upholstery is plastic. Light fixtures throughout house are plastic arcs held by ceiling battens

A WARM AND SUNNY CLIMATE is obvious in every line of this wide-open Florida house. A minimum of space is enclosed — and even that minimum literally flows into the outdoor living areas.

As the plot plan opposite shows, the house consists of two wings, connected only on the exterior. The wings are angled at 90 deg to shelter a large central garden and to provide a smaller private garden at the rear. Both gardens as well as a spacious play area behind the bedroom wing are completely secluded: a high louvered fence shields the eastern end of the central garden; hedges and closely planted trees rim the southern and western edges of the site.

The house has no halls and no "front door." The main entrance is through an electrically operated gate at the southeastern end of the central garden; a brick-paved walk connects the gate with the living room terrace. There is no garage, nor even a carport: the car

Residence for

Mr. and Mrs. Edward Riley

Miami, Florida

Alfred Parker, Architect

*Living room terrace (left and above) is red brick; gallery of bedroom wing has red cypress floor. Exterior walls are vertical cypress siding. Breakfast bar is at one end of kitchen (plan next page)*

Ezra Stoller

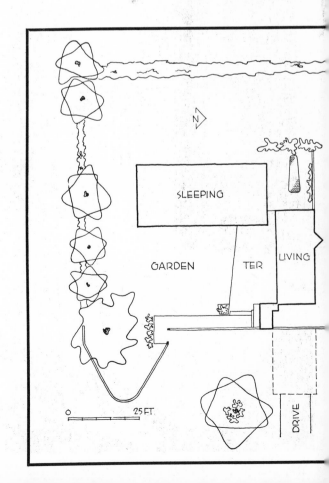

shelter (dotted lines on plan) at the end of the driveway is a yellow canvas awning laced to a frame of galvanized iron pipes.

Every room in the house except the laundry has direct access to the central garden — the two bedrooms via a gallery five steps up from the living room terrace. The difference in level increases the privacy of the bedroom wing and also adds visual interest to the enclosed garden area.

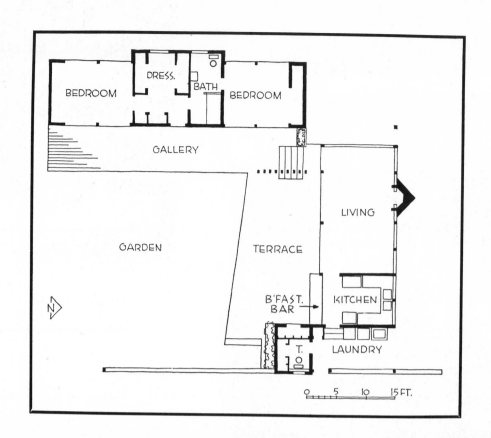

BEDROOM   DRESS.   BATH   BEDROOM

GALLERY

GARDEN   TERRACE   LIVING

B'FAST. BAR →   KITCHEN

T.   LAUNDRY

N

0   5   10   15 FT.

*Opposite page: despite proximity of neighboring houses, garden is remarkably private thanks to high fence and strategic planting; louvered fence has base of red brick pavers. Left: living room chimney is de-emphasized by strip windows above and glass wall at one side. Below, left: kitchen, like other rooms in house, is minimum in size. Below: view from laundry steps through length of living room wing to private garden at rear*

Ezra Stoller

*Above: space between wings at rear of house was planned for private garden with a small pool, not yet installed. Amount of wood used on interior of house — particularly in bedroom wing — is pleasant surprise considering Miami location. Bedrooms are connected by dressing room as well as gallery*

Ezra Stoller

# WHERE ECONOMY GUIDED DESIGN

*Weaver Residence, Thornwood, N. Y.*
*Warren Wilson Weaver, Architect*

THE SITE OF THIS HOUSE, in a sparsely populated area of Westchester County, invited a plan that would incorporate the surrounding countryside with the interior: economy dictated a simple design. Result: a small, flat-roofed rectangle that seems much more spacious than it actually is, due to the large glass areas that seem to bring the outside in. A central utility core, flanked on either side by kitchen and bath, is the main economy factor. An oil burner, also part of a packaged utility core, furnishes hot air heat. Additional warmth results from natural solar heat penetrating the abundant glass areas. The foundation is concrete and concrete block. Floors are linoleum and carpet over ¼-in. plywood.

Lighting is from the ceiling in the living area; wall mounted light troughs illuminate the bedroom wing. Many built-in units, designed and built by the architect-owner, provide adequate storage facilities for the occupants and permit flexible furniture arrangements. Interior walls are cedar siding with redwood stain, fir plywood and mahogany plywood. Cedar siding on the exterior has been painted brick red — a harmonious contrast to the green environment. The house is connected to the garage by a screened porch, which, convenient to the kitchen, serves as a pleasant dining area in the summer. The well lighted garage contains a workshop area at window end and built-in shelves line the outer wall.

*The house is so oriented as to permit the winter sun to penetrate the large glass areas. Eyebrow overhang provides wind and glare protection*

Unbroken wall is master bedroom and dressing room. Clerestories and strip window in garage afford unusual light for workshop area

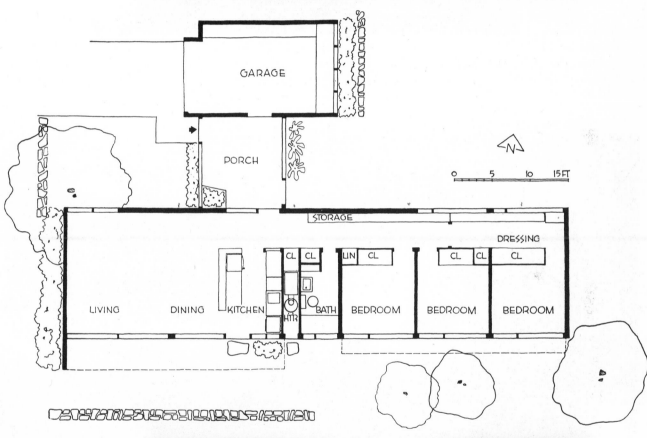

GARAGE

PORCH

N

0    5    10    15 FT

STORAGE

DRESSING

LIVING    DINING    KITCHEN    CL  CL    LIN  CL    CL  CL  CL

HTR    BATH    BEDROOM    BEDROOM    BEDROOM

Entrance to house is through connecting porch. Extension of garage at extreme left was designed for built-in storage shelves

Joseph W. Molitor

**Redwood-stained** cedar siding on end wall of living room is enriched only by a painting of Weaver child. Window wall admits excellent light

**Dining end** of living room with kitchen in background has storage room-divider designed by the architect. Door is main entry from porch. Turquoise carpeting complements tangerine wall

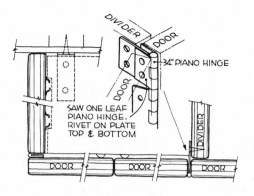

Detail *illustrates piano hinge used on architect-designed closet. Finished unit, below, separates master bedroom from dressing room*

**Bedroom wing corridor** has plywood cabinets along outer wall. An attractive and useful keynote is added by primary colors on unit openings

**Brush drawings** by Soriano provide the principal decor in daughter's bedroom. Walls are blue and yellow. Storage unit extends under window

Joseph W. Molitor

*Philip C. Johnson, designer*

*Landis Gores, associated*

# A CONNECTICU

Ezra Stoller

**House for Richard Hodgson**

UNLIKE THE FUSSY RESTLESSNESS that characterizes many houses, this design achieves both clarity of expression and a feeling of repose. The essential horizontality of the structure's disciplined envelope and its quiet colors contribute to its restfulness, as does the simplicity with which masonry and voids have been handled. Careful attention to detail, insistence on a high standard of craftsmanship, and the studied articulation of surfaces and materials are all factors in the effect of orderliness.

To achieve the necessary separation of living, sleeping and service areas in a manner maintaining privacy with a minimum cutting apart of these elements, they have been arranged in U shape about a landscaped patio which becomes the major focus of the design. Such a scheme yields some of the amenities of the attenuated "zoned" plan in more compact form. A future bedroom wing to the east will complete the scheme.

The roof construction consists of wood joists framing into steel girders supported by masonry and the four interior steel H-columns. With the exception of a small area, the floor slab is built on grade and contains hot-water radiant heating coils.

The ceiling is white acoustical plaster; the walls pale gray glazed brick, white plaster or oak; the floor is black ceramic tile; all exposed metal is painted charcoal gray.

**New Canaan, Connecticut**

Ezra Stoller

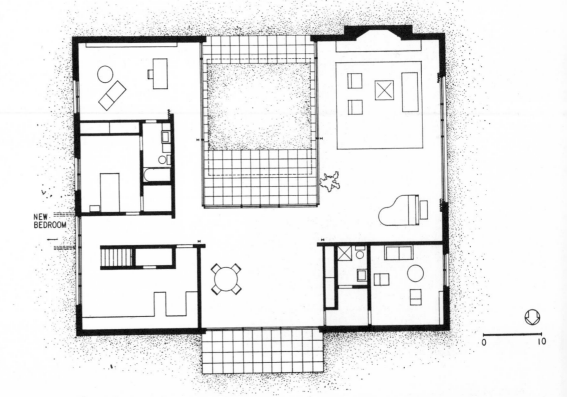

NEW
BEDROOM

0          10

The house is located on a wooded hillside overlooking the valley to High Ridge beyond and is
set in a clearing on a gently raised earth plat-
form much in the spirit of the historic podium.
The three pictures above, right and left, show
the exterior elevations from as many directions

Glazing the plane on axis with the patio gives the interior direction and yields a "through" effect

Ezra Stoller

**THE HODGSON HOUSE, NEW CANAAN, CONNECTICUT**

Looking into the patio from the clearing, top left

View from entry into living room, bottom left

Large recessed fireplace is living room focus, below

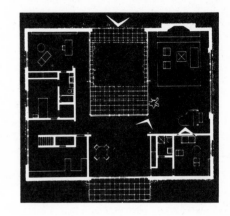

Robert C. Cleveland

# ...PERVISION OF CHILDREN

*French Residence, Fillmore, Calif.; Chalfant Head, Architect*

THE BASIC REQUIREMENT in the design of this house was to incorporate two separate living areas into the interior plan — one for the adults and one for the children. This need was met by placing a combination family dining and play room between the adult living room and the kitchen. Supervision of the play area from both kitchen and living room is possible due to wall openings between the rooms, as seen in photos on following pages.

The house is set on a sloping plot in mountain foothills, and entry is made from a paved ramp leading from the motor court, which is slightly higher in level. A patio in the front at floor level is afforded privacy from the road through various high plantings along a low wall. Built on a modular system, the house rests on a concrete slab foundation. Exterior finish is natural finished redwood with yellow trim. Roof is built-up composition topped with heat-deflecting white gravel. Heating is by radiant panel system with copper tubes embedded in slab. Photos on these pages depict slanting driveway from the road above, sheltered ramp to entry and various other exterior views of house. Relation of house to irregular shaped plot is indicated at right.

*How harmonious living for families with children can be achieved through careful planning. Such an example is this house with a centrally located "family room" for supervised play and dining*

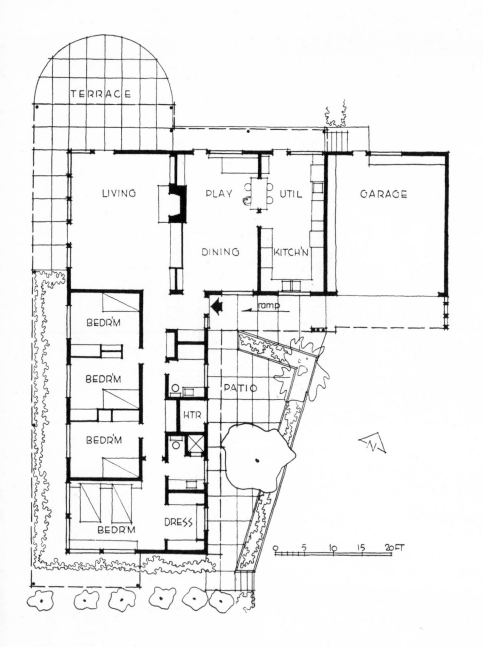

## FRENCH RESIDENCE

*A house need not be large and portentous to accommodate both adults and children in peaceful and uncluttered surroundings.*

**A)** *Adult living room with pass-through to "family room" for simplified entertaining has built-in cabinet wall containing radio-phonograph and loudspeaker above.* **B)** *Master bedroom is at far end of bedroom wing, affording privacy and quiet to adult members of family; has built-in desk, bookcases and trays below sliding wood casements, found throughout house.* **C)** *Kitchen is adjacent to children's play area and is well lighted—both naturally and artificially.* **D)** *Snack center is conveniently located between kitchen and play area.* **E)** *View of play space and main dining area from snack bar shows spaciousness of "family room." Section of living room seen at pass-through on opposite cabinet wall*

**A**

**B**

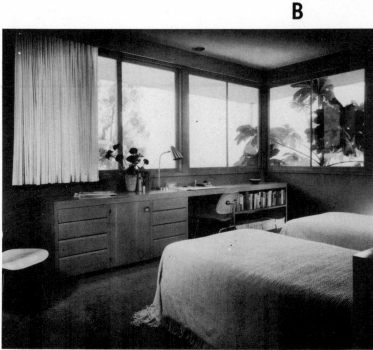

C

Robert C. Cleveland

D

E

COMPACTNESS was the first requirement for this Los Angeles house: the owners, a couple with no children, had lived for a number of years in a residential hotel, with no household responsibilities whatever, and were understandably anxious to keep maintenance problems to a minimum. The most notable feature of the plan, however, is not the compactness but the deep-in-the-country privacy achieved on a city lot.

The house is on a low hill with a distant view of the ocean and the city. The site, irregular in shape and not too large, slopes steeply downward toward the view; existing eucalyptus and fir trees — most of which were saved — provided natural landscaping, and were used to frame the house. Well distributed

planting space outside the terrace windows and along the brick motor court wall takes the place of a garden.

At the owner's request the house is two stories in height, with living rooms and maid's quarters on the ground floor and the two master bedrooms upstairs. Both living and dining rooms open to a curved terrace protected from the winds by the high brick wall and the house itself, but freely overlooking the view to the south. The master bedrooms, each with its own dressing room and bath, share an 8-ft-wide balcony, partly screened for fly-less sunbathing.

The structural frame of the house is based on a 6 ft-4 in. module with steel posts and wood beams. Exterior walls are stucco and redwood siding.

Semicircular brick wall of motor court is integrated into design of house, gives complete privacy to all living areas and shields terrace from wind. Doors in wall (opposite page) lead to terrace at one end, yard at other. Exterior of house is colorful: salmon brick wall, redwood siding, aluminum window frames, brilliant coral wood panels between first and second story hall windows. Aluminum sheet canopy connects house with garage

# CITY RESIDENCE BOASTS COUNTRY PRIVACY

*House for Mr. and Mrs. Gustav Dann*
*Hollywood Hills, Los Angeles, California*

*J. R. Davidson, Designer*

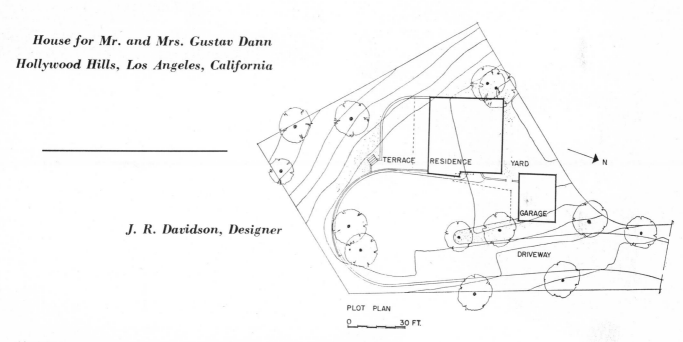

PLOT PLAN
0    30 FT.

Julius Shulman

Steepness of site at south and east necessitated retaining wall for the filled-in terrace of living and dining rooms. From just a few feet below the house only the second floor is visible. Screen on bedroom balcony is plastic, on steel frame. Window frames are lemon yellow

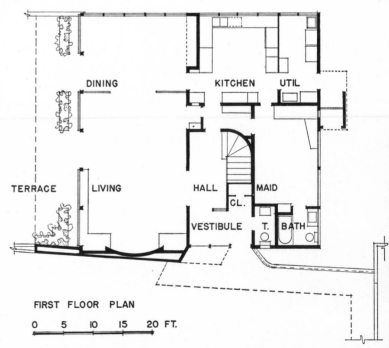

*Left: main entrance is from motor court; door is wood, painted eggplant to contrast with salmon of brick wall; lower windows are ribbed glass, entrance paving is Arizona flagstone. Above: view of terrace through door to motor court; bedroom balcony has high railing of cypress siding for privacy*

FIRST FLOOR PLAN

0   5   10   15   20 FT.

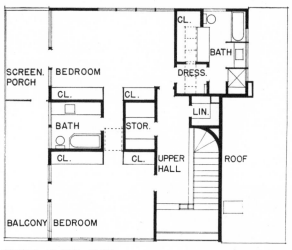

SECOND FLOOR PLAN

Julius Shulman

*Terrace overlooks the city — but distantly, over the trees.*
*Paving is cement with exposed aggregates and brick liners*

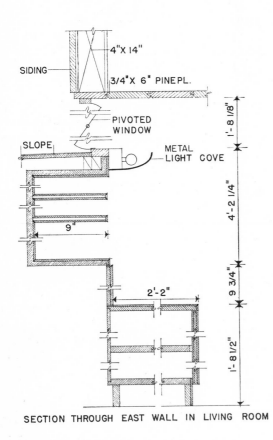

SIDING

4" X 14"

3/4" X 6" PINE PL.

PIVOTED WINDOW

SLOPE

METAL LIGHT COVE

1'-8 1/8"

4'-2 1/4"

9"

9 3/4"

2'-2"

1'-8 1/2"

SECTION THROUGH EAST WALL IN LIVING ROOM

*Above and below: living room looking toward terrace. Ceiling is pine T & G; east wall and low cabinet under window are natural elm, waxed. Floor is cork, rug is light cocoa colored loop. All lights are recessed, and a light cove runs the length of the east wall above the book shelves and cabinets (section at left above)*

Two sliding screens of woven wood close off dining room when desired. Dining room floor and ceiling are same materials as in living room. Buffet wall is paneled in elm, waxed; lights are built into buffet ceiling. House is heated by radiant panel, in floor on lower level, in ceiling on upper

Julius Shulman

## CITY RESIDENCE—COUNTRY PRIVACY

*Left: vestibule floor is Arizona flagstone, ceiling is coral-painted plywood, wall is light gray. Small wood mesh screen separates vestibule from hall. Below: second floor hall uses low storage cabinets with planting box at one end as railing above stairs. Carpet here and on stairs is cocoa, wall at left is painted to match. Two-story hall windows are clear glass; draw curtains are bamboo weave*

Bath between two master bedrooms is key to second-floor versatility: owners can spread out over entire floor or assign a completely separate suite to guests. Medicine cabinet (detail, below left) is flush with wall, has sliding mirror door. Glass jalousies at windows; asphalt tile floor, light yellow walls, gray lavatory top. Each of three baths (including maid's on ground floor) has electric wall heater

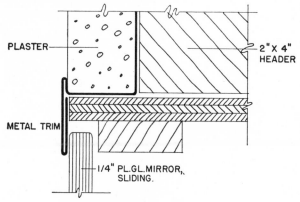

PLASTER

2" X 4" HEADER

METAL TRIM

1/4" PL.GL.MIRROR, SLIDING.

DETAIL OF MEDICINE CABINET HEAD HALF SIZE.

Storage space, excellent throughout the house, is particularly good on second floor. Each bedroom has two large clothes closets, and the master bedroom (left) has in addition a much larger closet off the dressing alcove plus built-in storage drawers and shelves. Upstairs hall also has linen closet and large shelf-lined storage room

# AN ARCHITECT'S HOUSE IN THE COUNTRY

*The Winston Elting House, Libertyville, Ill.*
*Schweiker and Elting, Architects*
*Franz Lipp, Landscape Architect*
*S. R. Lewis & Associates, Heating Engineers*

SEVERAL DECADES AGO we can imagine the design for a country house on a scale as large as this spending most of its resources in creating an impressive façade. Today, as evidence that the new architecture has begun to assert its philosophy, we see this big house quietly spreading out in an open, informal arrangement rather than rearing up to impress its neighbors and insult the landscape. Here we find a concern for a more sincere approach to planning, orientation, expression of structures and materials, with the emphasis on pleasantly informal country living and quietly expansive entertaining. The result is a house that skillfully identifies its owner with the rusticity of the countryside by way of a sophisticated contemporary design.

The owner says, "The decision to move from the suburbs and build in the country was made . . . not only because of a wish to participate in country life as much as a farm of 21 acres would permit, but also because of the opportunity for planning freedom and experimentation that an architect-owner combination permits."

The site was obvious to the owner from the beginning; a slight rise in the fields boasting four fine old oak trees. The approach from the west (above) reveals a gracious one-story house that reaches a lean finger out between

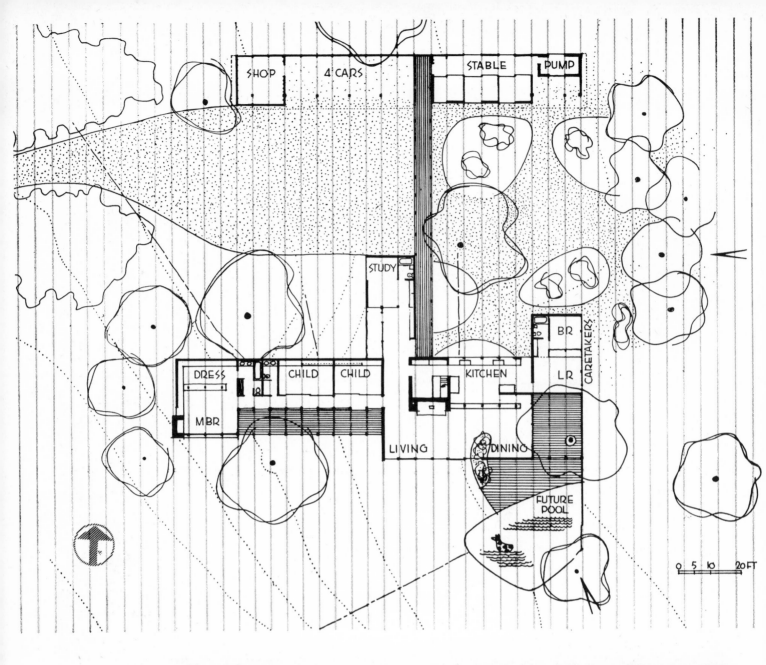

SHOP  4 CARS  STABLE  PUMP

STUDY

BR

CARETAKERS

DRESS  CHILD  CHILD  KITCHEN  LR

MBR

LIVING  DINING

FUTURE
POOL

0  5  10  20 FT

140

*Left page: house from southeast looking towards terrace.*
*Above: covered walkway to the stable building at right*

the trees to link itself with the low-lying stable to the north. This horizontality gives the structure a feeling of serenity and relates it subtly to the softly rolling meadowlands about.

The large photo on page 138 more or less synthesizes the interior character achieved; the open feeling, the exposed structure within its modular discipline, the natural wood ceilings, walls and floors. This theme is consistently repeated throughout, the wide use of wood being a personal choice of the owner which dictated the structure and to a lesser extent the plan.

The plan is organized about a structural system of beams and columns spaced 5 ft 4 in. on centers; is open and elongated in character, representing the culmination

of the architects' development of the "outward-looking" plan, which includes the outdoors by open exposure rather than by making it an inherent part of the building itself. The main house is essentially a long east-west rectangle with south exposure, entered near its center. It features a 48-ft long area subdivided by an indoor-outdoor planting box into living and dining spaces which expand into a tree-shaded terrace which in turn will be flanked by a future pool. The bedroom wing, semi-closed on three sides, has large sliding glass panels opening to a covered gallery looking out over the meadows beyond. The servant couple's apartment faces east to a view and adds the bonus of pleasing orientation and privacy to its occupants' salaries. A study-guest

*Living-dining room floor is 2 by 4 fir planks in natural finish separated by ⅜ in. fir strips stained dark. East terrace beyond and at same level has a floor of similar planks with open ⅜ in. joints. Resulting effect is the apparent continuation of floor pattern indoors and out*

room and bath is located north of the entrance for privacy near the point where the 46-ft covered walk to the stable begins. The stable building houses stalls for three horses, a garage, car shelter, feed room, hay storage and pump house.

The exposed structural post and beam system is of Douglas fir timber with a 2-in. plank roof and finish floor, also of fir. Non-load bearing interior and exterior walls are of 1 by 12 rough-sawn redwood. All doors, millwork and built-in cabinets are of redwood. The terraces and covered walk have open plank floors. The built-up roof on plank insulation is topped by the same red gravel that is used for the entrance court and paths

of the garden court separating house and stable. Split granite boulders were carefully selected and placed in the forms for the concrete fireplaces and chimneys to create a pattern furthering the relation of the house to the land. Fixed glass panels are double glazed; movable panels are plate glass.

Natural ventilation is achieved by sliding glass doors on the south exposure, bottom-hinged glazed sash to the north, and by hinged wood panels behind louvers in the master bedroom and servants' apartment. Heating is by low velocity forced warm air split into four zones, each thermostatically controlled, with individual outlets also manually regulated.

## ARCHITECT'S COUNTRY HOUSE

*Above: view from a child's bedroom looking across gallery to the view*

*Right: large sliding translucent panels create the effect of two rooms which are separated from but still remain a part of the bedroom gallery*

*Right page, top: the master bedroom is ventilated by hinged panels below the fixed glass — contains its own fireplace and desk-dressing counter*

*Right page, bottom: bathrooms feature redwood in natural finish. Thick slab containing recessed lavatories is moisture-resistant laminated maple*

Bill Hedrich, Hedrich-Blessing

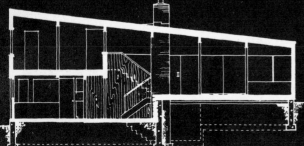

The natural slope dictated a split-level scheme, which creates pleasantly varied spaces under the simple roof pitch. From the middle level living room one can walk up seven risers to the bedroom gallery or down seven risers to the dining area

Tom Ballenger

Richard Garrison

# A THREE-LEVEL HOUSE IN MASSACHUSETTS

*Hugh Stubbins, Jr., Architect*

THREE NATURAL ELEMENTS — slope, woods and view — jointly influenced the shaping of this house in section. The site, dotted with tall white pine trees, is a small knoll falling gently off to the south towards a pleasant pond. Nearing the house from the west one sees the large flat roof over the carport and entrance approach. This dominant horizontal relates the house to the flatness of the pond and creates a strong contrast to the verticality of the pines as well as the trapezoidal shape of the main element of the house.

The land slope from west to east dictated the split-level arrangement of the principal rooms, which are disposed in an essentially rectangular plan sheltered by a roof that pitches to oppose the incline of the ground.

Entrance is at living room level, which looks down on the view over the higher terrace. From this middle level one can walk either up seven risers to the bedrooms or down seven risers to the dining-kitchen area, which opens in turn to a lower terrace.

The resulting interior provides a sensation of great spaciousness together with visual change from one area to another; the whole pulled into unity by the canted plane of the roof above.

An eight-foot structural module is maintained throughout; north and south beams are 4 by 14s supported on 4 by 6 posts. The disciplined structural system is everywhere apparent, both indoors and out; its expression serves to make the concept more valid.

Richard Garrison

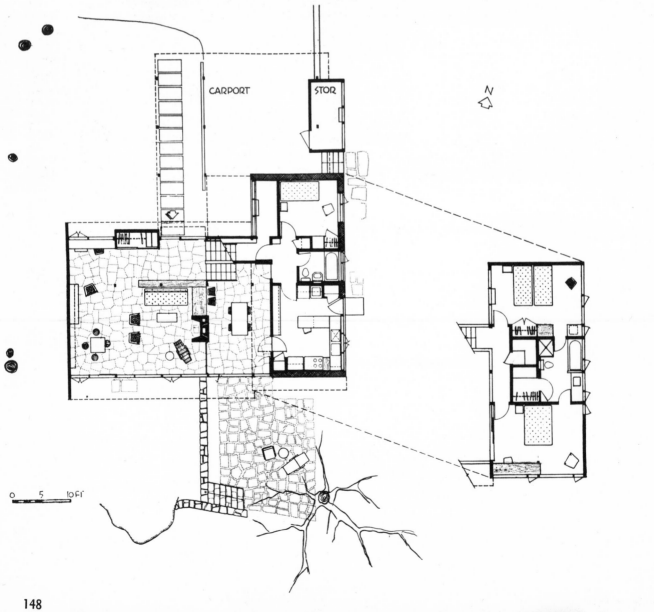

CARPORT   STOR

N

0   5   10 FT

Under the carport and entrance shelter at the north side of the house, both the structure and its disciplined modular organization are expressed. Exterior walls are vertical redwood siding stained with creosote; fascias and frames for doors and windows are painted white. The entrance door is located at the middle or split-level and leads to the living area

The architect's plan, left page, points up the open character of the interior of the house. Separations are achieved by visual blocks or by low elements with either glass or voids above. This results in a series of spaces that seem to interflow and expand, both vertically and horizontally

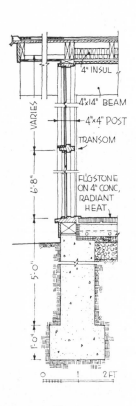

4" INSUL

4"x14" BEAM

4"x4" POST

TRANSOM

FL'GSTONE ON 4" CONC, RADIANT HEAT

VARIES

6'-8"

5'-0"

1'-0"

0    1    2 FT

Richard Garrison

*Entry, above, is separated from the main living area by a low cabinet and connected to the remainder of the house by the stairway*

*Bedroom, above, and living room, below, look out to the south and afford a view of the pond, while the dining area (p. 146) opens to the same view from a still different elevation. This constant tying together of house and site from different station points provides both variety and a means of orienting oneself with the plot*

H. O. Wiseman

Entrance to house (below) is from cul-de-sac on east side of property. Brick walk leads past planting box window in living room to south terrace. Opposite page: brick wall and planting box divide south terrace into ''public'' and ''private'' areas

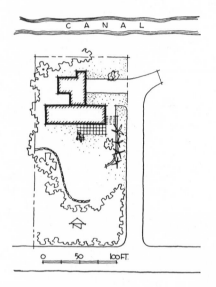

Joseph W. Molitor

152

# DESIGNED FOR ENTERTAINMENT

*Shreveport, Louisiana*     *William B. Wiener, Architect*

A CORNER LOT, sloping gently from west to east, determined both the placing of this house and the use of two levels. A family consisting of the architect, his wife, and teen-aged son and daughter — all interested in outdoor and indoor entertaining, gardening, hunting and fishing — determined the plan, location of the patio and close relationship between carport and "private" entrance.

This is a real family house, as the plan (next page)

shows. Its living and sleeping areas are almost two distinct houses, separated not only by level but also by a 12-in. fire wall. Each wing has its own heating, ventilating and air conditioning units. Living, dining and game rooms can be used either individually or together, depending on the family's entertainment program; a party given by one person in no way interferes with activities of another, or with the early-to-bed ideas of someone else.

Joseph W. Molitor

H. O. Wiseman

## WIENER HOUSE

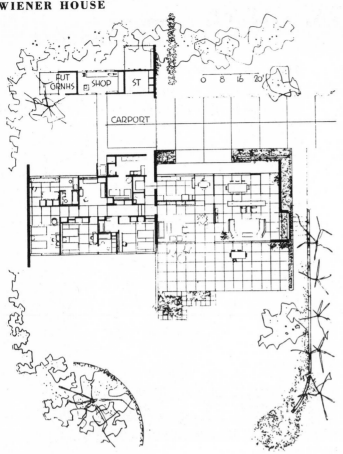

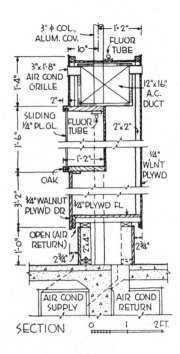

3" φ COL.,
ALUM. COV.
FLUOR
TUBE
10"
1'-2"

3"x 1'-8"
AIR COND
GRILLE
12"x16"
A.C.
DUCT
2"

1'-4"

SLIDING
¼" PL.GL.
FLUOR
TUBE
2"x 2"

1'-6"

1'-2"
¼"
WLNT
PLYWD

OAK

3'-2"

¾"WALNUT
PLYWD DR
¾" PLYWD FL

OPEN (AIR
RETURN)
2"x 4"
2¾"

1'-0"

2¾"

AIR COND
SUPPLY
AIR COND
RETURN

SECTION 0 1 2 FT.

*Main entrance (above) is at north corner of house; short hall leads past dining room to living room. Family has private entrance adjacent to carport. Right: game room*

Arrangement and height of partitions in living room wing are adroitly worked out to provide for family's varying entertainment needs. Living room (above) and game room (below) can be used separately or together; ceilings are acoustically treated. Game room has door (left below) opening directly to bedroom corridor. Air conditioning ducts for this wing are in door-height cabinet (left in photo above; detail opposite)

Joseph W. Molitor

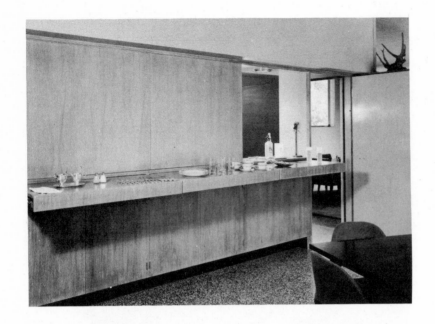

All interior and exterior walls and partitions (except east, west and center) are non-load bearing, which permitted completion of roof and pouring of terrazzo floors before partitions were in place. Most partitions contain storage or service facilities. Game room (previous page and top left) has built-in service counter at one end of cabinet wall, as useful for large buffet suppers involving entire living-dining wing as for informal entertaining in game room alone. Cabinets frequently combine display space with enclosed storage, as in dining room (left, below) and in kitchen-breakfast room area (below). Interior walls are plywood, brick and plaster, used in combination in "public" areas to emphasize flow of room into room

Joseph W. Molitor

Although entire house was planned around the varying needs and habits of a four-member family, bedroom wing especially reflects family and individual requirements. Entire wing is on higher level than living area for maximum privacy, has separate heating and air conditioning systems and a private entrance. Each bedroom has its own bath and specially designed storage units; master bedroom (right) also has large dressing room. All three bedrooms have direct access to rest of house and to carport. Family interest in hunting and fishing resulted in gun and tackle closet at end of private entrance hall, conveniently close to carport. Guest room (below) can be left open for family use or closed off by sliding panel for guests

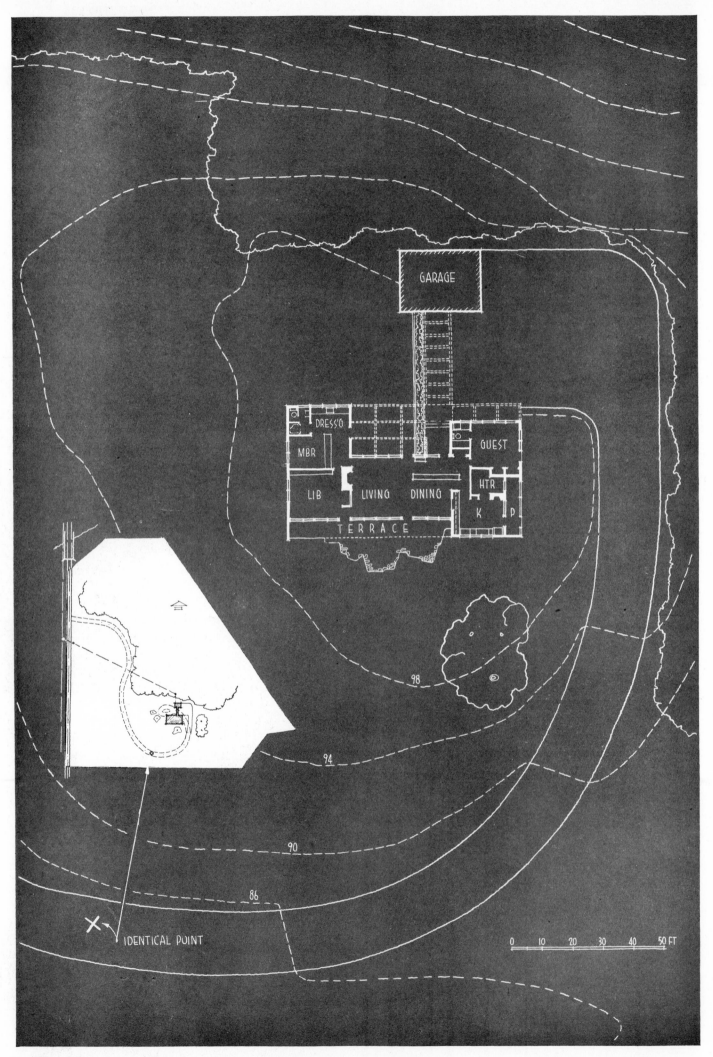

GARAGE

DRESS'G

MBR

GUEST

LIB

LIVING

DINING

HTR

K

P

TERRACE

98

94

90

86

IDENTICAL POINT

0   10   20   30   40   50 FT

# GOOD LIVING FOR SMALL SERVANTLESS FAMILY

*Residence of J. Spencer Bell*

*Charlotte, North Carolina*

*A. G. Odell, Jr. and Associates, Architects*

Joseph W. Molitor

## RESIDENCE OF MR. AND MRS. J. SPENCER BELL

A HILLSIDE SITE with contrasting views in opposite directions was a chief problem in the planning of this house. Both views — a densely wooded ravine to the north and a sloping meadow to the south — merited living room outlook; the solution was a central living room wing running east-west, flanked by bedroom and service wings.

The owners, a couple whose only child is grown, wanted a house easy to care for and enjoy without servants. Out of this requirement came such features as a kitchen unusually large for a house of this size, with a fireplace and grill; a library-den quickly closed off from the living room by a ceiling-high sliding door; and a two-way cabinet between kitchen and dining room which can double as a bar.

Construction is wood frame on concrete foundation. Exterior walls are redwood, interior walls are plywood and plaster. Floors are sawed random rectangular slate, sand rubbed.

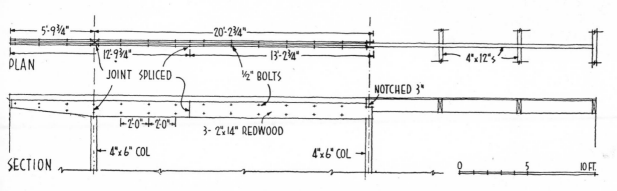

PLAN

|← 5'-9¾" →| |← 20'-2¾" →| 4"x12"s

|← 12'-9¾" →|← 13'-2¾" →|

JOINT SPLICED     ½" BOLTS

NOTCHED 3"

SECTION

|← 2'-0" →|← 2'-0" →|  3- 2"x14" REDWOOD

4"x6" COL          4"x6" COL

0      5      10 FT.

Joseph W. Molitor

*Living room (opposite) has north and south walls largely of glass to take advantage of contrasting views; wide overhang protects south side (detail above). Top right: library-den. Right: dining room is separated from entrance vestibule by free-standing cabinet providing miscellaneous storage and housing a three-speaker record player and radio*

Storage space is exceptionally good throughout the house, but especially in kitchen (left) and master bedroom suite (right and below). Storage unit separating bedroom and dressing room reaches neither floor nor ceiling, permits ventilation straight through house. Both master bedroom and guest room (bottom, opposite) have direct access to outdoors, and guest room has its own patio

Joseph W. Molitor

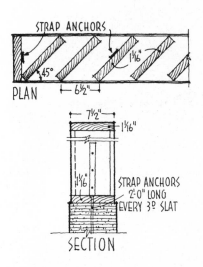

**DETAIL OF LOUVERED FENCE**

Julius Shulman

## HOUSE FOR TWO
## EXPANDS FOR GUESTS

*Residence of Mr. and Mrs. Maurice L. Heller*
*Beverly Hills, California*

*Richard J. Neutra, Architect*

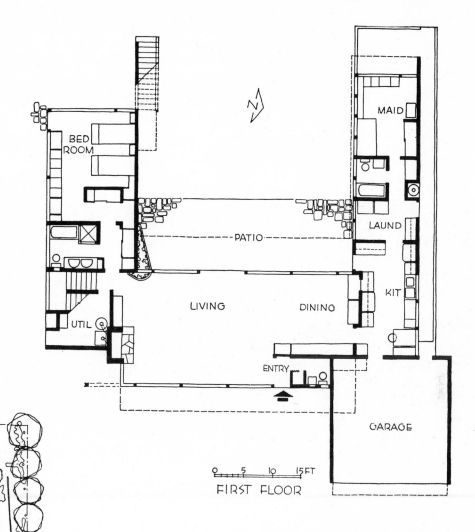

PATIO

BED ROOM

MAID

LAUND

KIT

LIVING

DINING

UTIL

ENTRY

GARAGE

0 5 10 15FT

FIRST FLOOR

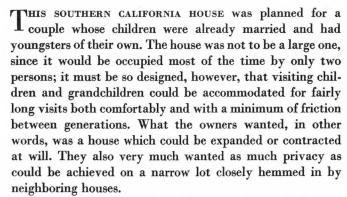

PLAY AREA

FUT. POOL

0 50FT

THIS SOUTHERN CALIFORNIA HOUSE was planned for a couple whose children were already married and had youngsters of their own. The house was not to be a large one, since it would be occupied most of the time by only two persons; it must be so designed, however, that visiting children and grandchildren could be accommodated for fairly long visits both comfortably and with a minimum of friction between generations. What the owners wanted, in other words, was a house which could be expanded or contracted at will. They also very much wanted as much privacy as could be achieved on a narrow lot closely hemmed in by neighboring houses.

The solution was a U-shaped house straddling the lot and enclosing a patio. A two-story bedroom wing provides a guest suite (plan on page 170) which can be closed off when not occupied; the maid's room and bath, at one end of the northern wing, can be similarly shut off when not in use — or could be pressed into service as an extra guest room if required (it has its own small patio and entrance). The rest of the house is not too large for a family of two, and is easily cared for.

# HOUSE FOR TWO EXPANDS FOR GUESTS

Remarkable privacy was secured for every part of both house and gardens. The front is protected from the street by trees and bushes through which winds a stepped walk leading to the main entrance. Planting and high windows shelter the two side wings, which in turn protect the patio. A broad lawn edged by planting stretches from the flagstone terrace outside the living room wing all the way to the rear of the lot where the play area is almost out of sight and sound.

The location of the play area is typical of the care with which the house and grounds were zoned to keep one age group from disturbing another. The second

floor guest suite can be reached directly from the lawn, and the children's bunk room is over the utility room at the opposite end of the bedroom wing from the master suite. Living room and patio are far enough from the bunk room to permit late entertaining without risk of disturbing visiting grandchildren.

Just as much care went into simplifying housekeeping in the main part of the house. Much of the furniture is built in. The kitchen is all-electric, compact and planned in close cooperation with the owners; a door connects it with the garage putting the family car within a few feet of kitchen counters.

Western wall of living-dining wing is a series of floor-to-ceiling glass panels, some sliding to open area to flagstone terrace and patio. Dining room table, designed by architect, can be lowered in few seconds to coffee-table height (below) to incorporate dining area into living room. Built-in settee on east wall of living room is below bank of high windows with mitered glass corner planned for view of tall old fir tree. Fireplace is Arizona flagstone, built-in buffet and other furniture are birch. Large mirror above buffet brings garden view to everyone at dining table

*Master bedroom achieves maximum privacy by solid wall on patio side, high windows on opposite; end wall facing rear lawn, however, is glass from floor to ceiling. All furniture is built in. Owner's fold-down drafting table (bottom of page) is on second floor, at door to roof terrace*

HOUSE FOR TWO EXPANDS FOR GUESTS

*Above: living-dining area is undivided, and separated from patio only by glass walls; floors are cork, ceiling 1 by 4 T & G. Below: upper-floor guest suite is connected with patio by outdoor stairs with open risers, protective railings*

Julius Shulman

## HOUSE FOR TWO EXPANDS FOR GUESTS

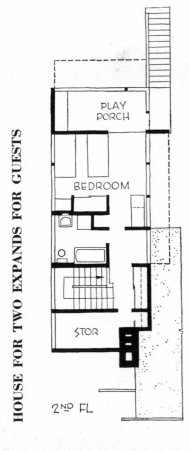

PLAY PORCH

BEDROOM

STOR

2ND FL

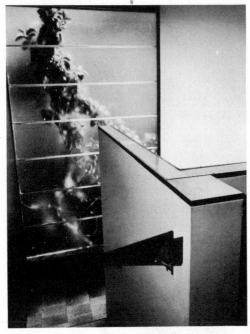

Second-floor guest suite overlooks patio except for children's bunk room-storage room, which is at far end of wing, above utility room. Porch is partly glassed in, partly screened; it doubles as bad weather playroom and guest sitting room. Stair landing (above) is enlivened by trans-luscent window framing gnarled vine which is silhouetted at night by exterior

170

# COUNTRY HOUSE ON LONG ISLAND

*Residence for K. L. Rawson*

*Serge P. Petroff and Harvey P. Clarkson, Architects*

THIS competently designed country house, although intended for a somewhat more formal way of life and for year-round occupancy, still reflects much of the same spirit as a weekend house in its use of natural materials and open planning in its major living areas. Principal rooms are oriented to face the view afforded by the hilltop site and have exterior walls made mostly of glass. The front entrance of the house is on the opposite side of the building and passes through a cloister-like patio formed by the guest room-library wing and the children's wing. This separation of sleeping quarters affords a great amount of privacy to each of the occupants. The patio itself may be opened out to the front lawn by raising a series of venetian blind panels in the enclosing wall. The house has natural-finished vertical siding, white trim.

Joseph W. Molitor

The U-shaped plan (below) has centralized living and service areas, flanked by three sleeping wings. Actual living space is extended by a sheltered terrace and a patio

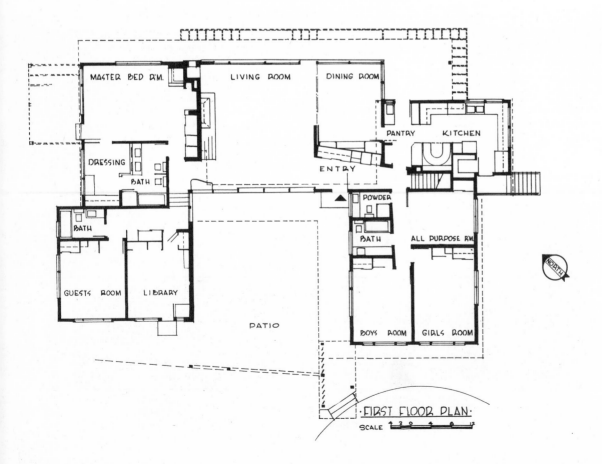

MASTER BED R'M.    LIVING ROOM    DINING ROOM

DRESSING                          PANTRY    KITCHEN

BATH                              ENTRY

                                  POWDER

BATH                              BATH    ALL PURPOSE R'M.

GUESTS ROOM    LIBRARY

PATIO    BOYS ROOM    GIRLS ROOM

NORTH

·FIRST FLOOR PLAN·

SCALE

# RAWSON HOUSE

*Photos at far left and below, center show the northeast façade, with its covered terrace off the glass-walled living rooms. The kitchen also opens directly on the terrace to simplify service for outdoor dining*

*Privacy is gained for patio at front of house by venetian blinds hung on wood frame (above and below, left). Front entrance is shown directly below*

Joseph W. Molitor

The large living room (above) opens on both the terrace and the patio,
is separated from dining area by folding partition. Study, guest room
and master bedroom (below) open off corridor by fireplace wall

Well-equipped kitchen (right) opens directly
to dining room and dining terrace, both of
which are visible in the photo above

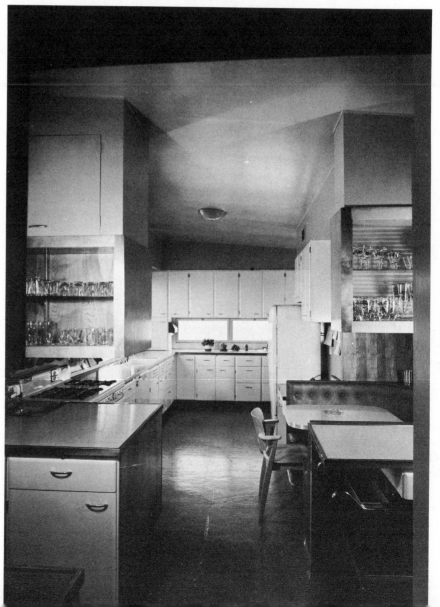

# CANTILEVERED DECK ADDS LIVING SPACE

*Residence for Mr. and Mrs. H. E. Lunken*
*Cincinnati, Ohio*
*Carl A. Strauss, Architect*
*Henry Fletcher Kenney, Landscape Architect*

WHILE this site's sharp hillside slope presented building difficulties, a view of the Ohio River and convenience to downtown Cincinnati determined its selection. Maximum advantage of the view is taken by the living and dining rooms' south wall of glass and by the cantilevered deck which runs the entire length of the house. To avoid a steeply-graded driveway, the carport was built at a higher level than the house; a flight of steps from the carport leads down to the main living floor. (See plan on page 178.)

In the living-dining area, walls and ceilings are ⅜-in. ash panelling, fireplace is painted brick, and floors are cork. The screened-in porch has a canvas-deck floor, while asphalt tile is used for floors throughout the service area. The maid's room and bath in this section are also cantilevered, since a sewer directly beneath made the use of footing walls impossible.

On the lower floor, deck acts as a sunshade for the south side of the house; master bedroom opens to terrace. Floors on this level are also cork; walls are painted plaster. Ceilings of acoustic tile are used in the hall, children's rooms and baths.

House is steel frame and wood joist construction; upper floor covered with vertical, gray-stained redwood boards. Rear walls, which act as retaining walls, are reinforced concrete, while front wall is brick and glass. Roof is built-up tongue and groove. A 7½-ton unit provides air conditioning.

Bill Hedrich, Hedrich-Blessing

*Left: sliding steel frame doors form part of glass wall, open on 10-ft deck. Below, left: radio-record-book cabinet also acts as stair railing. Below, right: two-way fireplace separates living and dining areas*

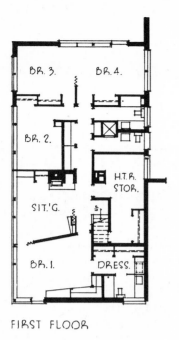

BR. 3.  BR. 4.

BR. 2.

SIT.'G.

BR. 1.  DRESS.

H.T.R. STOR.

FIRST FLOOR

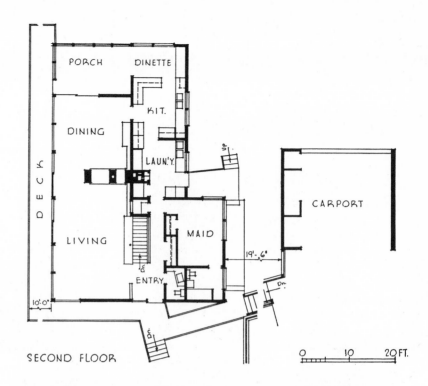

DECK

PORCH  DINETTE

DINING  KIT.

LAUN'Y.

LIVING  MAID

ENTRY

CARPORT

UP

19'-6"

10'-0"

0  10  20 FT.

SECOND FLOOR

**LUNKEN HOUSE**

Above: children's rooms are divided by folding wall, have outside door to play yard. Above, right: sitting room has folding partitions to hall and master bedroom, can be used as a guest room. Right: kitchen cabinets are stained birch; pass-through counter serves dinette

# HOUSES OF THE NORTHWEST

THE HOUSES in this study were deliberately chosen to illustrate several points about domestic architecture in the Northwest. One is the persistence of an early cottage form, which with its pitched roof, wide overhang and large window areas is well suited to the climate. Another is skill in the use of wood; wood is used naturally, but boldly too, delicately also, and, yes, lovingly, for the great timber here was the first attraction of this country, and brought Scandinavians and their skills and habits. These houses also show plainly the acceptance and digestion of contemporary international currents of thought. They show too the Northwest willingness to experiment, as using flat roofs occasionally in spite of the ubiquitous shingles and shakes. Interiors in these houses are especially interesting, sometimes for conflicting reasons. First, the architects generally have more control over interiors than is usual with small houses. On the other hand, it seems a rare instance where the architect can dictate strictly modern furniture. The independence of the typical family with respect to faddish notions is plainly evident in the mixtures of furnishings, urns and Indian and Japanese art objects. Thus does the individuality of this country assert itself.

---

# HOUSE THAT TYPIFIES NORTHWEST ARCHITECTURE

*Paul Von Bergen House, Portland, Ore.*

*John Storrs, Designer*

HERE IS A HOUSE that typifies the Northwest, on a typical site, with a typical view (30 miles toward Mt. Jefferson). The cottage form is evident, though it just happens that Mr. Storrs did not grow up with it — he came from an eastern university and adopted the Northwest country on his first trip there. Here he had favorable clients, a young couple with educated tastes and (as the interior photographs will show) an enthusiasm for Japanese art. There is no attempt here at a Japanese house, but rather for a proper use of the site. The trees come close, both to give a near focus for the views and to form a shield against the rain-filled winds from the southwest.

The house is of standard frame construction. The three cased beams supporting the roof are exposed throughout, and form the head details for glass and doors. The two outside beams are 7 ft from the floor, and a horizontal line is carried around the interior at this level, marking door heads and the top of walls between rooms; thus the ceilings are continuous planes extending over the diverse room activities. As a princi-

ple, instead of throwing open the whole to the outside, the designer sought a visual change of pace, emphasizing interior and near exterior views as well as framing the distant view toward the mountain.

Chas. R. Pearson

*". . . some basic characteristics common to people and architecture. A straightforwardness n*

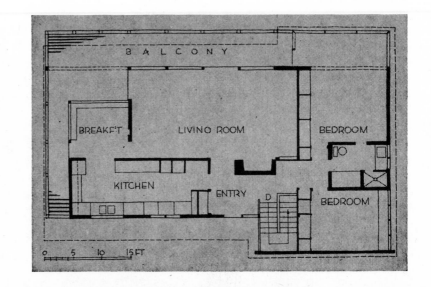

Von Bergen house has garage at upper level, joined to house by covered walk; covered balcony on two sides, toward the view. Bedroom has store front window construction to open it fully (below), is screened on this side by trees close to house

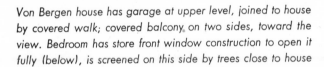

*o full of pretense, an appreciation and fondness for the sophisticated and polished . . .*

Chas. R. Pearson

*". . . at the same time a liking for the rustic natural texture of rough hewn wood and stone"*

John S. Detlie

interiors of Von Bergen house maintain a 7-ft line, the level of cased beams and height of solid partitions, for continuity. Glass is used above partitions, to close off certain areas but maintain one ceiling

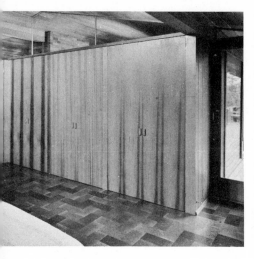

Cedar is used for most interiors — walls, ceilings, doors, even in stair well and bathroom. Floors are cork throughout. This monochromatic coloring sets off furnishings and Japanese oils, plates, carvings

*. . . came a reaction against things as they were and a desire to design for the country . . .*

Kitchen maintains same woods used through rest of interiors, though birch was used for the cabinets. Kitchen is closed off from entry and from living room by 7-ft partition, is open to breakfast room

*"... maybe not a 'machine for living' but a building that would fit a better way of life"*

## A HOUSE WITHOUT STAIR

*Thomas Dixon House, Portland, Ore.*

*Van Evera Bailey, Architect*

*Robert E. Kremers, Structural Engineer*

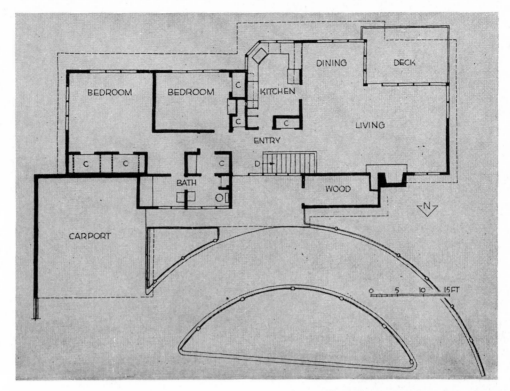

# N A VERY STEEP SITE

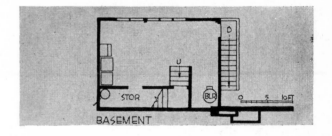

BASEMENT

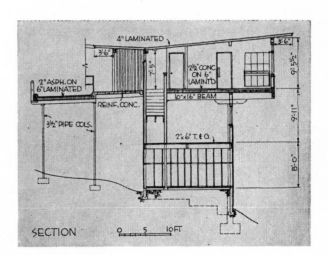

SECTION

THIS HOUSE could scarcely be called typical of its architect's work, but does seem to emphasize the daring with which Northwest architects tackle their sites and their buildings. Basic objective was a house to obviate the scrambling up and down steps, and analysis proved the soundness of the idea. Preliminary designs were done with the usual steep drives and steps, but the grade would make winter driving hazardous. Also heavy retaining walls would be necessary, and a foundation heavy enough to resist pressure of road backfilling. Costs would equal those for steel pipe supports. The circular driveway is in fact a structural necessity to give the house on stilts lateral stiffness. The arch of the driveway, with supporting beams running into the house, transfers horizontal stresses to the curb retaining wall on city right of way. The building line of the house could not encroach on the street, but the driveway could. The family has no children, otherwise the house on stilts would be unthinkable.

In plan, all living areas are located to take advantage of the sweeping views and the sunshine to the south. The roof slopes upward on this side to permit the sun to enter in winter months, though the architect comments frankly that this might have been overdone, as "actually there is too much sun on winter days, when there is any."

*Floor is built up of 2-by-6's on edge, covered with 2½ in. of concrete. Floor is supported by solid 10-by-16 wood beams, on 3½-in. pipe columns. Driveway is also laminated with 2-by-6's on edge, with 2-in. asphalt*

*". . . that would enliven the gray days of winter and share the exterior country in summer .*

*. . buildings that would shed the rain and yet permit the sun to infiltrate the interior"*

Paul Thiry

Open and airy feeling of the Dixon house is heightened by the use of painted plaster walls and light asphalt tile flooring, also light-colored drapes and furniture. Ceiling is exposed edges of 1-by-2 and 3-by-4 rough-sawn fir boards laminated to form structural roof

# A HOUSE WITH LARGE SPACES, LONG VISTAS

*W. W. Wessinger House, Portland, Ore.*

*Walter Gordon, Architect,*

AN UNUSUAL AMOUNT of client conference went into this house, extending over two years. The owners, a young couple, three children, one maid, wanted an "uninhibited space sense" which here clearly means a great big house with great big views both inside and out. The outside views nature provided lavishly — two rivers to the north, sunsets to the west, at an elevation of 1000 ft above Portland's downtown. So there are large panes of glass on virtually all sides. The family also wanted activity separations — dead-end living room, shielded sleeping rooms, separated kitchen and play wing, in a house they could add onto or subtract from. They wanted terrific storage cabinets, and they wanted natural woods, "large and varied amounts of it." This would seem to be a clear invitation to the architect to let himself go, so the house has some fairly dramatic touches. The huge living-dining room (more than 40 ft long) is open, except for a screen, to the glazed entry. A continuous ceiling of longitudinal, natural hemlock takes the slope of the roof and emphasizes the length and openness of the room. The lines of the house give a strong feeling of serenity, though as one poetic observer said, "a contemporary home with long sweeping planes which lift with the rise of the land, finally cresting, like a wave, into a sharp-pitched roof." Anyway, it's a consistent roof line, with accents.

*". . . Puget Sound with its incomparable variety of ocean, sound and strait, inlet, river and*

Dearborn-Massar

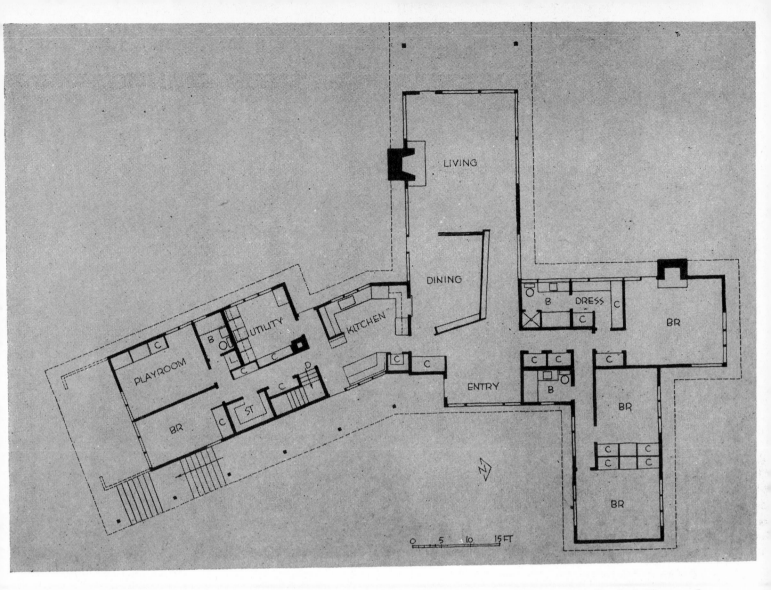

*lake, of plains rising to snow-capped mountains, forests and shore of salt-bleached driftwood. . .*

*The long, low roof lines are strongly favored in Northwest designs; this house is actually larger than it appears, and uses space with a lavish hand*

While some of the interiors are of plaster, this house shows its Northwest heritage with extensive use of wood — sloped ceiling of long hemlock boards, birch for cabinets and screens. Exterior of resawn vertical T & G Western Red Cedar

*"The region is too young to have developed any architectural style . . . none was imported . .*

# COMPACT HOUSE WITH A SENSE OF SPACIOUSNESS

*Alden Mason House, Seattle, Wash.*

*Victor Steinbrueck, Architect*

Not all houses in the Northwest are as big as the outdoors; this one is a model of compactness. Propped up on the side of its lot, its basement exposed to the front, its porch cantilevered toward the sidewalk, it still manages to look imposing as well as interesting. Commentary on the Northwest: you seldom see monotonous rows of dinky houses — the sites absolutely prevent monotony and the architects (builders too) lean strongly to a quality of individuality. This house uses its space effectively: the porch, serving as a screen for living and dining room windows, permits full and open glass toward the street. The living room, though small, has very usable space since there is no traffic through it. The progressively open plan from living room to dining room to kitchen adds spaciousness but still screens kitchen. Altogether the house seems much larger than it actually is.

The architect found many ways to develop the sense of size. That is, by the way, the purpose of the wing walls extending out at the ends. These were used to complete the form of the house and to extend the interior spaces outward. The narrow exterior siding (1/2 by 4 in., bevel, Western Red Cedar) tends to scale the house, and is much cheaper than wide boards. Also the siding was colored with tile red stain, which has an assertive quality. Inside the ceiling and soffits are all 1-by-4, T & G, V-joint cedar, and floors are in one-color dark asphalt tile, the uniformity tending to add to apparent spaciousness.

If all that seems a great deal of design for a house that cost (1949) the owner $9000 (he painted it himself), take it as an added commentary on the Northwest: there it is not strange for architects to work on such small houses, and give them studied care.

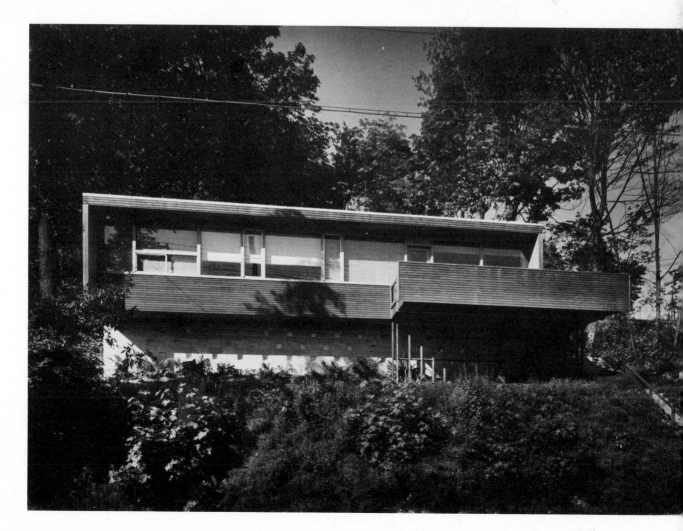

*"Neither in the architecture nor the people is there a sense of urgency, or of mission . . .*

The Mason house, though small, has many devices that give it a strong individuality, an assertive quality. The extended end walls are useful in this respect, especially on the interior, where they have the effect of extending the interior spaces

Dearborn-Massar

The plan utilizes its areas effectively; the living room loses no space for circulation purposes, though there is possibly a small sacrifice in this, in making it necessary for guests to walk past the living room windows. Openness of living, dining, kitchen makes space efficient

". . . with awakened enthusiasm a certain elemental directness and simplicity is established . . .

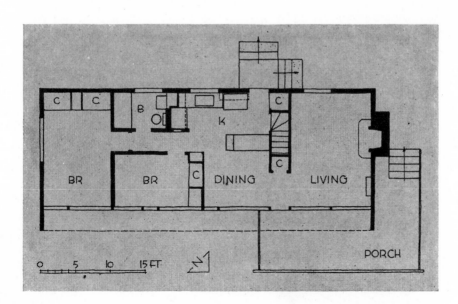

*. wood, stone, plant material in contrast to the mannered machine-ordered substances . . .*

All ceilings and soffits are 1-by-4 T & G, V-joint Western Red Cedar, finished only with a clear preservative sealer. Floors are all in a single color, dark asphalt tile, this uniformity being calculated to add apparent spaciousness

"*With the new vocabulary of expression is a guard against the hurry to formalize anything*

Dearborn-Massar

*Plywood walls were stained by adding pigment to a clear preservative sealer: blue in dining room, light yellow in the child's room, white in the hall, light olive green on kitchen cabinets. Cabinets and doors were varnished in addition. Kitchen counter tops are crimson red vinyl, with hardwood nosings*

*nto a set design ritual . . . and a note of capricious humor is often used . . ."*

John S. Detlie

# PLANNED FOR OUTDOOR LIVING ON A HILLSIDE

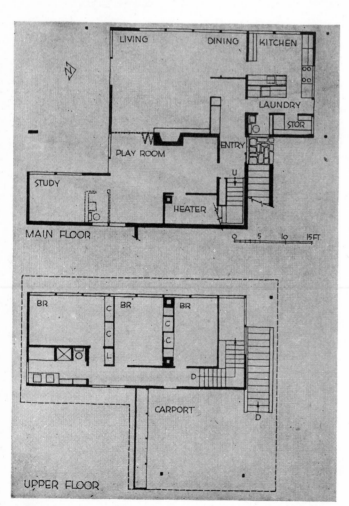

*Jack Wolf House, Mercer Island, Wash.*

*Robert H. Dietz, Architect*

IN THE PUGET SOUND AREA it doesn't seem odd that an architect would help his clients choose a site so steep that the house goes downhill in steps — it would be difficult not to select such a site. At any rate the architect did help select it, and designed the house as a sort of grandstand facing the view of Lake Washington and the floating bridge; all principal rooms face the lake. The owners wanted easy access to outdoors from living rooms; this was easy to arrange by making this part of the house the lower level — main entrance is at bedroom level.

The clients gave the architect no trouble about style, wanting only that the house exemplify good architecture for the Northwest and satisfy their needs and desires. It won a local A.I.A. honor award in 1950 for the best contemporary house.

The entire house is of wood. Interior finish is primarily hemlock and vertical grain fir and fir plywood. Fireplace is of local Wilkeson stone.

*"The area is no longer isolated from the rest of the nation, and consequently we are economica*

*The living room below is a good example of contemporary design in the Northwest, a post and beam house of local materials and largely wood interiors, wood ceiling and beams*

*ist as close to all products as, say, Chicago. This is producing here a standardization . . .*

# A LARGE HOUSE WITH A PUGET SOUND APPROACH

*Thomas David Stimson House, Seattle, Wash.*

*Paul Thiry, Architect*

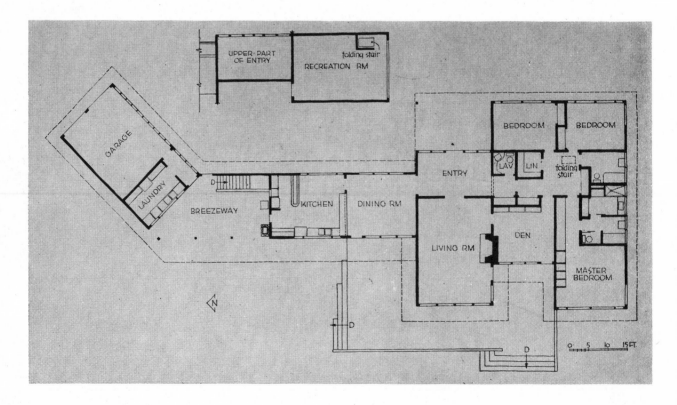

*"This could result in a different form of architecture than found elsewhere . . .*

A LARGE HOUSE, self sufficient in its mannerisms, this one provides an interesting commentary on Northwest domestic architecture. It certainly shows an acceptance and assimilation of the modern approach, but there is no evidence of effort to assert any stylistic doctrine. It is true that, knowing the architect and his clients here, one might find touches that would establish a sympathy for Japanese forms and furnishings, but there is nothing very insistent about it. In the main the distinguishing forms of this house come from the problem at hand, a problem frequently encountered in the Puget Sound area. The house, high on a promontory, faces west, toward the views of the Sound and the Olympic Mountains, also toward the afternoon sun and the glare from the water. There is also wind and rain from the southwest. Roof overhangs, plantings around the terrace, but at the same time the huge glass areas, illustrate the efforts commonly made to enjoy the views and the sun but exercise some control when the weather turns unpleasant. The house is of frame construction, conventional stud wall and rafters. Exterior is vertical T & G cedar, left to weather naturally; roof, hand split shakes. Window frames are wood, soffits and gables are fir painted in color (Chinese red and yellow).

Chas. R. Pearson

*ecause it would result from a real cause . . . that cannot be satisfied by materials alone."*

Robert H. Dietz

Entrance hall, dining room and library
are walled with walnut plywood, though
most interior walls are of plaster. Floors
are mostly carpeted, though in entrance
hall and dining room the flooring is traver-
tine slabs in random pattern. Colors
throughout are subdued browns, tans and
mistletoe. Furnishings mostly Oriental

Living room, den and master bedroom
face the views, the western sun and
the weather. The overhangs at the
gable ends, the glass wind screen,
the plantings, are all designed to take
advantage of the views and the sun
but control the glare and the winds

*". . . an indigenous architecture borrowing from the high primitive arts and structures of*

Chas. R. Pearson

*lians; conscious of the simple mill sheds that were built in open span for timber sizes . . .*

# A HOUSE NOT FOR A VIEW, BUT FOR A FAMILY

*William J. Bain House, Seattle, Wash.*
*William J. Bain and Harrison Overturf, Architects*

SETTING OUT, like the previous one, with no very pronounced stylistic mission, this house did have a definite objective, having nothing to do with a view or a weather problem. Here the view is a landscaped creation, and the objective to suit the fairly lavish desires of a large family. A detailed explanation of all features would involve a rather personal acquaintance with the family, down to their menus. Briefly, their wants here involve a great deal of entertaining, by adults and by young people too; anticipation of entertaining married sons and daughters and possibly small fry. Music here and there, for dancing or just for listening. Cooking here and there, too, notably barbecues in the recreation room. Many of these activities are calculated to flow outward to either front or rear terraces, hence the heavy screening by plantings, and the extensive paving and stone work. Though large, the house and the landscaping are planned for easy management without servants — lawn areas are small, planting is mainly hardy shrubs, flower beds are limited, could be dispensed with entirely.

*". . . conscious of the faraway land of Japan whose topography is similar to our own — whose*

From the barbecue fireplace in the recreation room to the furnishings of the living room, the interiors were designed, like the house itself, for very comfortable living, its expression one of exuberance

Chas. R. Pearson

*eople have developed a post and lintel architecture free in adaptability of form . . ."*

Paul Thiry

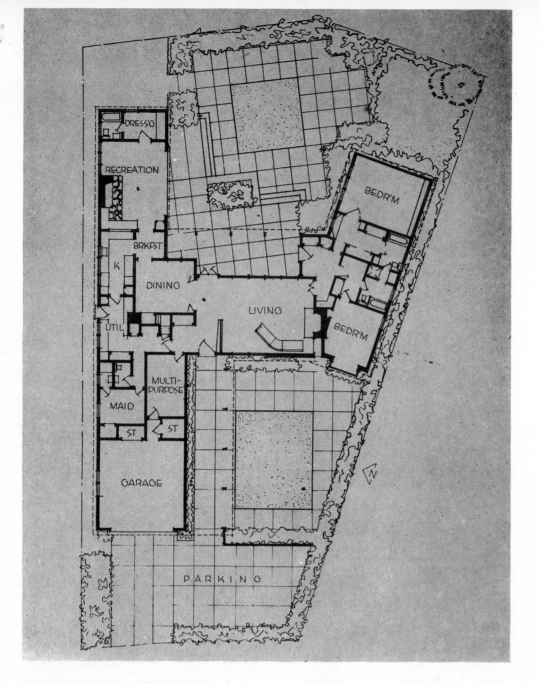

Though the emphasis of the Bain house is on family, there are but two bedrooms. This is explained by the fact that the two sons have left the household and no longer require permanent rooms. The closet space, though, was designed to store their things, and the recreation room works nicely as a bedroom, for times when they come home, with or without wife and other impedimenta. This room is mainly useful, however, as a center for entertaining; it connects to kitchen via sliding door over counters

*". . . setting of the region presents a problem of magnitude which does not suggest a solution*

# THE CLIENT SPECIFIED HOSPITALITY

*Carl Erickson House, Hunts Point, Wash.*

*Young & Richardson; Carleton & Detlie, Architects*

IT WAS THE DESIRE of the owners," reports the architect, "to have a home which would take full advantage of Lake Washington and a panoramic view of Seattle on the horizon and at the same time yield itself gracefully to the general terrain and character of Hunts Point. The character of the architecture was to suggest formality and dignity with a warm sense of hospitality, and yet achieve in appropriate areas complete infor-mality." The house presents its dark side to the visitor, hence the intricate arrangement of planes, beginning with the carport and taking the eye downward past a landscaped entrance rookery to the entrance. On the side facing the lake the house is much more restrained; here the house aligns its rooms and opens itself toward the lake. The all-glass room jutting out is the kitchen, designed as an informal entertaining center.

Chas. R. Pearson

*much as a humbleness of approach and a vigorous statement of form and texture...*

Except for its generosity in the matter of space the plan accommodates fairly normal requirements. A special item is the large kitchen facing the lake, conceived as an informal center for the family or for close friends at cocktail time

## "The definitive nature of the artistic expression of the region is in the process of formulatio

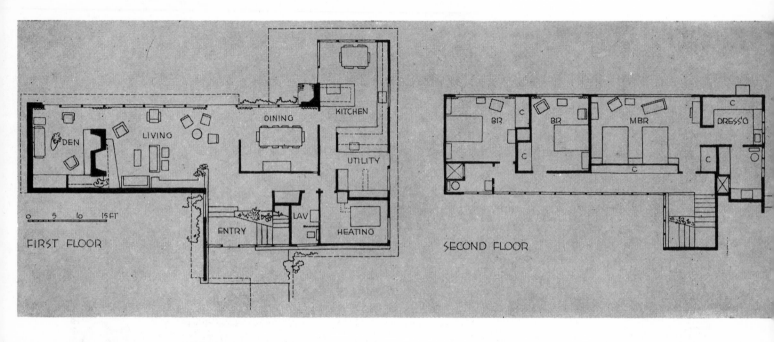

FIRST FLOOR

SECOND FLOOR

The more formal dining space is only partially closed off from the living room but is completely walled off from the entrance. In the background of this picture the den is handled in a similar way

*This kitchen center features—and that is the word for it—an indoor barbecue fireplace. There is one outside too, in fact it adjoins the one inside. Cook inside or outside and eat either place that suits your fancy best*

Chas. R. Pearson

*d has not yet emerged into a clear, graphical well grasped symbolism."*

John S. Detlie

# OPEN SPACE DESIGN SUITS WOODED SITE

*David Van Brown House, Hilltop Community, Wash.*

**Bassetti & Morse, Architects**

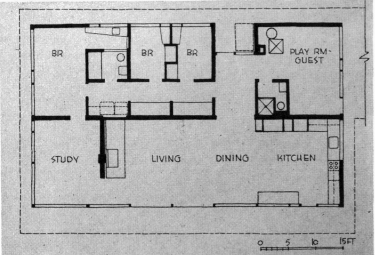

It would be interesting to quote at length from the architects' remarks about this house. But the quoting started with the clients, who sent the architects a long quote from Thoreau, starting: "I sometimes dream of a larger and more populous house, standing in a golden age, of enduring materials, and without gingerbread work, which shall consist of only one room . . ." Well, as the plan shows, the house could not exactly be vast, and ended up with three bedrooms, study, guest room. But the philosophy shows in the open cooking, eating, living space. It shows, too, in the materials. It is well known, around Puget Sound, that these architects have done much with the open space idea, and with the new materials. And now for the quotes from the architects: "We feel that this is one of the most difficult problems — this conflict between the use of new materials and, rarely, new forms and the avoidance of a self-conscious 'modernism' . . . Still I think that the Brown house is more successful than some others where we may have tried too hard."

*"It is in the people themselves that any impetus for definite architecture characteristic*

Chas. R. Pearson

Also from the architects: ''Wendell Lovett's furniture and fireplaces give it a sparkle inside which helps, even though they don't conform exactly with the 'barn and hearth' philosophy.''

*must spring, if the potentials of the setting, the climate and history are to be energized . . .*

Chas. R. Pearson

*". . . above all is a new, deep-felt appreciation of the majestic setting of Puget Sound."*

John S. Detlie

*In contrast with the openness of the living area, the bedroom space is on the efficient side. The corridor lined with huge closets serves also as a laundry—and where quite as conveniently?*

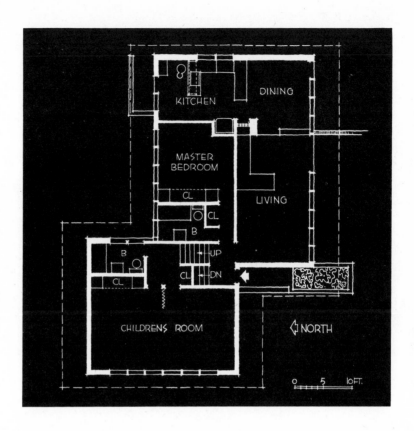

# ARCHITECT'S HOUSE IS ACTIVITY-ZONED

*Residence of Mr. and Mrs. Joseph Marlow*

*Denver, Colorado*

*Joseph Marlow, Architect*

*Louise Marlow, Associate*

THE TWO PHOTOS on p. 212 tell the story of this house: a gently sloping site used to achieve the desired interior heights. The three levels are "zoned" to separate adult and children's activities. Living and dining rooms, kitchen and master bedroom are on the main level; half a flight above is the children's bed-playroom and bath; half a flight below (not shown on plan) is the architect-owner's office, originally designed as a recreation room easily convertible into two additional bedrooms. Since the stairway is immediately adjacent to the main entrance, there is no cross-traffic between zones.

The house is set back 40 ft from the property line, giving the children ample outdoor play space. A flagstone terrace along the south side, not visible from the main entrance, provides a sheltered spot for adult entertaining.

Exterior walls are brick, interior partitions and ceilings are birch plywood, lacquered. Floors are concrete, waxed. The built-up roof has 4-in. rock wool insulation. Heating is radiant.

MARLOW HOUSE

Dining room is separated from kitchen (above) by serving bar,
from living room (below) by steps and two-way fireplace. Entire
south wall is floor-to-ceiling glass, with doors opening to terrace

# Index